Condensed Chicken Soup for the Soul

CONDENSED CHICKEN SOUP FOR THE SOUL

Jack Canfield, Mark Victor Hansen and Patty Hansen

Health Communications, Inc.
Deerfield Beach, Florida

Library of Congress Cataloging-in-Publication Data

Condensed chicken soup for the soul / [compiled by] Jack Canfield, Mark Victor Hansen,
  and Patty Hansen.
        p.   cm.
      "Condensed version of our first three Chicken soup for the soul books"—
  Acknowledgments.
      ISBN 1-55874-414-2
      1. Spiritual life—Anecdotes. 2. Parables. I. Canfield, Jack. II. Hansen, Mark Victor. III.
  Hansen, Patty. IV. Chicken soup for the soul.
  BL624.C657   1996
  158'.12—dc20   96-20596
                                                                              CIP

©1996 Jack Canfield, Mark Victor Hansen and Patty Hansen
ISBN 1-55874-414-2

Publisher: Health Communications, Inc.
          3201 S.W. 15th Street
          Deerfield Beach, Florida 33442-8190

Cover design by Nancy Kim Graves.

We thought that we
Had done it all
And then you asked
For Chicken Soup
"In small"

This book is lovingly dedicated to our readers, who have shared helpings of *Chicken Soup for the Soul* throughout the world . . . and to Gary Seidler and Peter Vegso, who have changed and enriched millions of lives—including our own.

Contents

2. LEARNING TO LOVE YOURSELF

3. ON PARENTING

4. ON TEACHING AND LEARNING

5. ON DEATH AND DYING

6. A MATTER OF ATTITUDE

7. OVERCOMING OBSTACLES

8. LIVE YOUR DREAM

9. ECLECTIC WISDOM

Acknowledgments

God created man because he loves stories.

Elie Wiesel

Although this book is small, a giant effort went into creating it to be a successful condensed version of our first three *Chicken Soup for the Soul* books. We would like to thank the following people for their contributions, without which this book could never have been completed:

First, and always, our children. Jack's children, Christopher, Oran and Kyle. Especially to Elisabeth and Melanie Hansen, who went without parents for the duration. Thank you for your emotional support, patience and understanding.

Thanks to Michelle Adams in Mark and Patty's office. Your tireless effort, unfailing good cheer, and your devotion are very much appreciated.

Michelle, we could not have done it without you. Thanks to Nancy Mitchell in Jack's office for her patient help obtaining permissions.

To all the people, too numerous to mention here, who worked for years typing, editing, compiling and writing the first three *Chicken Soup* books, in which all the condensed stories in this book are found.

Our gratitude to Christine Belleris, Mark Colucci and Matthew Diener, our editors at Health Communications, Inc. for their supreme efforts.

And especially to the contributors of the stories . . . without you, there would be no book. The generosity of heart that you have shared with our readers continues to warm millions of souls and change for the better millions of lives.

We have not included contributor biographies due to the limited space of this book. If you are interested in more information concerning our contributors, we encourage you to pick up a "big" *Chicken Soup* book. The volume of *Chicken Soup for the Soul* and the page number where each story appeared are in the "Permissions" section, found in the back of this book.

Introduction

It is with great pleasure that we offer this book of "condensed" *Chicken Soup for the Soul.* We have taken the most popular stories from *Chicken Soup for the Soul, A Second Helping of Chicken Soup for the Soul,* and *A Third Serving of Chicken Soup for the Soul* and condensed them into the essence of each story. Our intention is to provide you with a book that you can easily take with you—in a coat pocket or purse—and that can give you instant motivation and inspiration.

Whether you buy this book for yourself or as a gift for a friend or family member, rest assured that you have your hands on a book that will warm the heart, awaken the soul and rekindle the spirit. These stories will touch you at the deepest level and remind you of what is most important about being human.

Recent research indicates that when these stories are read, emotional and spiritual responses are evoked that have positive health benefits. Neurotransmitters are released in the brain to actually accelerate healing in the body. The stories will inspire you to reach out to friends and family with greater love and compassion, will comfort you in times of stress, and will delight you during times of triumph and joy. They encourage you to enthusiastically embrace your dreams and more willingly tackle the obstacles and challenges you will inevitably face in their realization.

We continue to be excited about the consistent feedback we receive through the thousands of calls and letters outlining the significant impact our books have made on readers. We receive 50 to 100 letters a day from people all over the world—Japan, Korea, the Philippines, Cuba, Germany, South Africa and Israel—as well as the United States and Canada, with comments like these:

"I was sent to jail in a 23-hour lock-down unit. I was thinking about suicide. As I was tearing up sheets, *Chicken Soup for the Soul* caught my eye and I began to read. As I read, I ran across people in the book that had it much worse than me. It inspired me to stay alive."

—*Pete, prison inmate*

"I lost my husband of 46 years recently. The shock and loss were terrible. My daughter in Las Vegas sent me a copy of *Chicken Soup for the Soul* and *A 2nd Helping of Chicken Soup for the Soul.* They have helped me to no end!"

—*D. E. Naylor, England*

"Though I am only 12, these books have forever left an imprint in my heart. Since I am learning and practicing the lessons taught in *Chicken Soup for the Soul,* I feel that the stories can be of greater value to the younger readers. *Chicken Soup for the Soul* has taught me of unconditional love, greater wisdom, death, dreams and goals, and many other things. I have learned to cherish what I have and never to take what I am offered for granted, one of life's most important lessons. I want to encourage anyone who has yet to read these books to jump on it right now."

—*Heather, Long Island, New York*

So . . . sit back, relax and enjoy the powerful journey you are about to begin as you share in the lives and stories of some very special people.

If after reading these stories you are moved to send us some of your personal favorites—either your own or something you've clipped from a magazine or newspaper—we'll gladly review them for possible inclusion in future volumes of *Chicken Soup for the Soul.*

Send them to:
Chicken Soup for the Soul
P.O. Box 30880 • Santa Barbara, CA 93130
fax: 805-563-2945
e-mail: soup4soul@aol.com
website: http://www.chickensoup.com

For more information about Jack or Mark: chickensoup@zoom.com

"I'm worried about Carl."

Stories are beings. You invite them to live with you.

They'll teach you what they know in return for being a good host.

When they're ready to move on, they'll let you know.

Then you pass them on to someone else.

A Cree Storyteller

1

ON LOVE

Love: The One Creative Force

*Spread love everywhere you go: First of all in your own house.
Give love to your children, to your wife or husband, to a next-
door neighbor. . . . Let no one ever come to you without leaving
better and happier. Be the living expression of God's kindness;
kindness in your face, kindness in your eyes, kindness in your
smile, kindness in your warm greeting.*

Mother Teresa

A college professor had his sociology class go into the Baltimore
slums to get case histories of 200 young boys. They were asked to write
an evaluation of each boy's future. In every case the students wrote,
"He hasn't got a chance." Twenty-five years later another sociology
professor came across the earlier study. He had his students follow up
on the project to see what had happened to these boys. With the
exception of 20 boys who had moved away or died, the students

learned that 176 of the remaining 180 had achieved more than ordinary success as lawyers, doctors and businessmen.

The professor was astounded and decided to pursue the matter further. Fortunately, all the men were in the area, and he was able to speak to each one. "How do you account for your success?" In each case the reply came with feeling: "There was a teacher."

The teacher was still alive, so he sought her out and asked the old but still alert lady what magic formula she had used to pull these boys out of the slums and into successful achievement.

The teacher's eyes sparkled and her lips broke into a gentle smile. "It's really very simple," she said. "I loved those boys."

Eric Butterworth

On Courage

Courage is resistance to fear, mastery of fear—not absence of fear.

Mark Twain

Many years ago, when I worked as a volunteer at Stanford Hospital, I got to know a little girl named Liza who was suffering from a rare and serious disease. Her only chance of recovery appeared to be a blood transfusion from her five-year-old brother, who had miraculously survived the same disease and had developed the antibodies needed to combat the illness. The doctor explained the situation to her little brother, and asked the boy if he would be willing to give his blood to his sister. I saw him hesitate for only a moment before taking a deep breath and saying, "Yes, I'll do it if it will save Liza."

As the transfusion progressed, he lay in a bed next to his sister and smiled, as we all did, seeing the color returning to her cheeks. Then his face grew pale and his smile faded. He looked up at the doctor and asked with a trembling voice, "Will I start to die right away?"

Being young, the boy had misunderstood the doctor; he thought he was going to have to give her *all* his blood.

Dan Millman

You will find as you look back upon your life that the moments that stand out, the moments when you have really lived, are the moments when you have done things in the spirit of love.

Henry Drummond

A Brother Like That

A friend of mine named Paul received an automobile from his brother as a Christmas present. On Christmas Eve when Paul came out of his office, a street urchin was walking around the shiny new car, admiring it. "Is this your car, Mister?" he asked.

Paul nodded. "My brother gave it to me for Christmas." The boy was astounded. "Boy, I wish . . ." He hesitated.

Of course Paul knew what he was going to wish for. He was going to wish he had a brother like that. But what the lad said jarred Paul all the way down to his heels.

"I wish," the boy went on, "that I could be a brother like that."

Paul was astonished. He asked the boy, "Would you like a ride?"

After a short ride, the boy turned and with his eyes aglow, said, "Will you stop where those two steps are?"

He ran up the steps. Then in a little while Paul heard him coming back, but he was not coming fast. He was carrying his little crippled brother. He sat him down on the bottom step, then sort of squeezed up against him and pointed to the car.

"There she is, Buddy, just like I told you upstairs. His brother gave it to him for Christmas and it didn't cost him a cent. And someday I'm gonna give you one just like it . . . then you can see for yourself all the pretty things in the Christmas windows that I've been trying to tell you about."

Paul got out and lifted the lad to the front seat of his car. The shining-eyed older brother climbed in beside him and the three of them began a memorable holiday ride.

That Christmas Eve, Paul learned what Jesus meant when He had said:

"It is more blessed to give . . ."

Dan Clark

True Love

Moses Mendelssohn, the grandfather of the well-known German composer, was far from being handsome. Along with a rather short stature, he had a grotesque hunchback.

One day he visited a merchant in Hamburg who had a lovely daughter named Frumtje. Moses fell hopelessly in love with her. But Frumtje was repulsed by his misshapen appearance.

When it came time for him to leave, Moses gathered his courage and climbed the stairs to her room to take one last opportunity to speak with her. She was a vision of heavenly beauty, but caused him deep sadness by her refusal to look at him. After several attempts at conversation, Moses shyly asked, "Do you believe marriages are made in heaven?"

"Yes," she answered, still looking at the floor. "And do you?"

"Yes I do," he replied. "You see, in heaven at the birth of each boy, the Lord announces which girl he will marry. When I was born, my future bride was pointed out to me. Then the Lord added, 'But your wife will be humpbacked.'

"Right then and there I called out, 'Oh Lord, a humpbacked woman would be a tragedy. Please, Lord, give me the hump and let her be beautiful.'"

Then Frumtje looked up into his eyes and was stirred by some deep memory. She reached out and gave Mendelssohn her hand and later became his devoted wife.

Barry and Joyce Vissell

In love the paradox occurs that two beings become one and yet remain two.

Erich Fromm

A Simple Gesture

Everybody can be great. . . . You only need a heart full of grace.
A soul generated by love.

Martin Luther King Jr.

Mark was walking home from school one day when he noticed that the boy ahead of him had tripped and dropped all the books he was carrying, along with two sweaters, a baseball bat, a glove and a small tape recorder. Mark knelt down and helped the boy pick up the scattered articles. Since they were going the same way, he helped to carry part of the burden. As they walked, Mark discovered the boy's name was Bill, that he loved video games, baseball and history, that he was having a lot of trouble with his other subjects and that he had just broken up with his girlfriend.

Mark went home after dropping Bill at his house. They continued to see each other around school, had lunch together once or twice, then both graduated from junior high school. They ended up in the same high school, where they had brief contacts over the years. Finally the long-awaited senior year came. Three weeks before graduation, Bill asked Mark if they could talk.

Bill reminded him of the day years ago when they had first met. "Do you ever wonder why I was carrying so many things home that day?" asked Bill. "You see, I cleaned out my locker because I didn't want to leave a mess for anyone else. I had stored away some of my mother's sleeping pills and I was going home to commit suicide. But after we spent some time together talking and laughing, I realized that if I had killed myself, I would have missed that time and so many others that might follow. So you see, Mark, when you picked up my books that day, you did a lot more. You saved my life."

John W. Schlatter

Puppies for Sale

A little boy appeared under the store owner's sign, "Puppies for Sale." "How much are you going to sell the puppies for?" he asked.

The store owner replied, "Anywhere from $30 to $50."

"I have $2.37," the little boy said. "Can I please look at them?"

The store owner smiled and whistled, and out of the kennel came five teeny, tiny balls of fur. One puppy was lagging considerably behind. Immediately the little boy singled out the lagging, limping puppy and said, "What's wrong with that little dog?"

The owner explained that it had no hip socket; it would always be lame. The little boy became excited. "That is the little puppy that I want to buy."

The store owner said, "No, you don't want to buy that little dog. If you really want him, I'll just give him to you."

The little boy got quite upset. He looked straight into the store owner's eyes, pointing his finger, and said, "I don't want you to give him to me. That little dog is worth every bit as much as all the other dogs and I'll pay full price. In fact, I'll give you $2.37 now, and 50 cents a month until I have him paid for."

The store owner countered, "You really don't want to buy this little dog. He is never going to be able to run and jump and play with you like the other puppies."

To this, the little boy reached down and rolled up his pant leg to reveal a badly twisted, crippled left leg supported by a big metal brace. He looked up at the store owner and softly replied, "Well, I don't run so well myself, and the little puppy will need someone who understands!"

Dan Clark

Heart Song

Once upon a time there was a great man who married the woman of his dreams. With their love, they created a little girl.

When the little girl was growing up, the great man would hug her and tell her, "I love you, little girl." The little girl would pout and say, "I'm not a little girl any more." Then the man would laugh and say, "But to me, you'll always be my little girl."

The little girl who-was-not-little-anymore left her home and went into the world. As she learned more about herself, she learned more about the man. One of his strengths was his ability to express his love to his family. It didn't matter where she went in the world, the man would call her and say, "I love you, little girl."

The day came when the little girl who-was-not-little-anymore received a phone call. The great man was damaged. He had had a stroke. He couldn't talk, smile, laugh, walk, hug, dance or tell the little girl who-was-not-little-anymore that he loved her.

And so she went to the side of the great man. When she walked into the room and saw him, he looked small and not strong at all. He looked at her and tried to speak, but he could not.

The little girl did the only thing she could do. She climbed up on the bed next to the great man, and drew her arms around the useless shoulders of her father.

Her head on his chest, she thought of many things. She remembered she had always felt protected and cherished by the great man. She felt grief for the loss she was to endure, the words of love that had comforted her.

And then she heard from within the man, the beat of his heart. The heart beat on, steadily unconcerned about the damage to the rest of the body. And while she rested there, the magic happened. She heard what she needed to hear.

His heart beat out the words that his mouth could no longer say. . . I love you, little girl . . . I love you, little girl . . . and she was comforted.

Patty Hansen

Who You Are Makes a Difference

One night a man came home to his 14-year-old son and sat him down. He said, "The most incredible thing happened to me today. I was in my office and one of the junior executives came in and he told me that he admired me and gave me a blue ribbon for being a creative genius. Imagine. He thinks I am a creative genius. Then he put this blue ribbon that says 'Who I am makes a difference' on my jacket above my heart. Then he gave me an extra ribbon and asked me to find somebody else to honor. As I was driving home tonight, I started thinking about whom I would honor with this ribbon and I thought about you. I want to honor you.

"My days are really hectic, and when I come home, I don't pay a lot of attention to you. Sometimes I scream at you for not getting enough good grades in school and for your bedroom being a mess, but somehow tonight, I just wanted to sit here and, well, just let you know that you do make a difference to me. Besides your mother, you are the most important person in my life. You're a great kid and I love you!"

The startled boy started to sob and sob, and he couldn't stop crying. His whole body shook, and he looked up at his father and said, through his broken tears, "I was planning on committing suicide tomorrow, Dad, because I didn't think you loved me. Now I don't need to do that."

Helice Bridges

Become a Steward of the Dream . . .

Give a Blue Ribbon to at least four other people to help create a foundation of acknowledgment for this generation and all generations to come.

I Don't Despair about Kids Today

Sometimes when I'm flying from one speaking engagement to another, I find myself sitting next to someone who's quite talkative. This is often a pleasant experience for me because I'm an inveterate people-watcher. I've heard stories of sadness, delight, fear and joy, and some that would rival those on *Oprah* and *Geraldo*.

Sad to say, there are times when I'm sitting next to someone who just wants to vent his spleen on a captive audience for 600 miles. It was one of those days. I settled in, resignedly, as my seatmate began his disquisition on the terrible state of the world with, "You know, kids today are . . ." He went on and on, sharing vague notions of the terrible state of teens and young adults, based on watching the six o'clock news rather selectively.

I gratefully disembarked the plane and bought a local paper on the way to the hotel. There, on an inside page, was an article that I believe ought to have been the front-page headline news.

In a little Indiana town, there was a 15-year-old boy with a brain tumor. He was undergoing radiation and chemotherapy treatments. As a result of those treatments, he had lost all of his hair. I remember how I would have felt about that at his age—I would have been mortified!

This young man's classmates spontaneously came to the rescue: all the boys in his grade asked their mothers if they could shave their heads so that Brian wouldn't be the only bald boy in the high school. There, on that page, was a photograph of a mother shaving off all of her son's hair, with the family looking on approvingly.

No, I don't despair about kids today.

Hanoch McCarty, Ed.D.

An Act of Kindness

You must give time to your fellow men—even if it's a little thing, do something for others—something for which you get no pay but the privilege of doing it.

Albert Schweitzer

President Abraham Lincoln often visited hospitals to talk with wounded soldiers during the Civil War. Once, doctors pointed out a young soldier who was near death and Lincoln went over to his bedside.

"Is there anything I can do for you?" asked the president.

The soldier obviously didn't recognize Lincoln, and with some effort he was able to whisper, "Would you please write a letter to my mother?"

A pen and paper were provided and the president carefully began to write down what the young man was able to say:

"My dearest mother, I was badly hurt while doing my duty. I'm afraid I'm not going to recover. Don't grieve too much for me, please.

Kiss Mary and John for me. May God bless you and father."

The soldier was too weak to continue, so Lincoln signed the letter for him and added, "Written for your son by Abraham Lincoln."

The young man asked to see the note and was astonished when he discovered who had written it. "Are you really the president?" he asked.

"Yes, I am," Lincoln replied quietly. Then he asked if there was anything else he could do.

"Would you please hold my hand?" the soldier asked. "It will help to see me through to the end."

In the hushed room, the tall gaunt president took the boy's hand in his and spoke warm words of encouragement until death came.

The Best of Bits & Pieces

Hugging Is

We need four hugs a day for survival. We need eight hugs a day for maintenance. We need twelve hugs a day for growth.

Virginia Satir

Hugging is healthy. It helps the immune system, cures depression, reduces stress and induces sleep. It's invigorating, rejuvenating and has no unpleasant side effects. Hugging is nothing less than a miracle drug.

Hugging is all natural. It is organic, naturally sweet, no artificial ingredients, non-polluting, environmentally friendly and 100 percent wholesome.

Hugging is the ideal gift. Great for any occasion, fun to give and receive, shows you care, comes with its own wrapping and, of course, fully returnable.

Hugging is practically perfect. No batteries to wear out, inflation-proof, non-fattening, no monthly payments, theft-proof and nontaxable.

Hugging is an underutilized resource with magical powers. When we open our hearts and arms we encourage others to do the same.

Think of the people in your life. Are there any words you'd like to say? Are there any hugs you want to share? Are you waiting and hoping someone else will ask first? Please don't wait! Initiate!

Charles Faraone

*L*ove cures people—both the ones who give it and the ones who receive it.

Dr. Karl Menninger

Do It Now!

In a class I teach for adults, I gave the assignment to "go to someone you love, and tell them that you love them."

At the beginning of the next class, one of the students began by saying, "I was angry with you last week when you gave us this assignment. I didn't feel I had anyone to say those words to. But as I began driving home my conscience started talking. Then I knew exactly who I needed to say 'I love you' to. Five years ago, my father and I had a vicious disagreement and never really resolved it. We avoided seeing each other unless we absolutely had to at family gatherings. We hardly spoke. So by the time I got home, I had convinced myself I was going to tell my father I loved him.

"Just making that decision seemed to lift a heavy load off my chest.

"At 5:30, I was at my parents' house ringing the doorbell, praying that Dad would answer the door. I was afraid if Mom answered,

I would chicken out and tell her instead. But as luck would have it, Dad did answer the door.

"I didn't waste any time—I took one step in the door and said, 'Dad, I just came over to tell you that I love you.'

"It was as if a transformation came over my dad. Before my eyes his face softened, the wrinkles seemed to disappear and he began to cry. He reached out and hugged me and said, 'I love you too, son, but I've never been able to say it.'

"But that's not even my point. Two days after that visit, my dad had a heart attack and is in the hospital. I don't even know if he'll make it.

"So my message to all of you is this: Don't wait to do the things you know need to be done. What if I had waited to tell my dad? Take the time to do what you need to do and *do it now!*"

Dennis E. Mannering

All I Remember

One day, while I was lying on a massage table in a dark, quiet room waiting for an appointment, a wave of longing swept over me. I checked to make sure I was awake and not dreaming, and I saw that I was as far removed from a dreamy state as one could possibly be. Each thought I had was like a drop of water disturbing a still pond, and I marveled at the peacefulness of each passing moment.

Suddenly my mother's face appeared—my mother, as she had been before Alzheimer's disease had stripped her of her mind, her humanity, and 50 pounds. Her magnificent silver hair crowned her sweet face. She was so real and so close I felt I could reach out and touch her. I even smelled the fragrance of Joy, her favorite perfume. She seemed to be waiting and did not speak.

I said, "Oh, Mother, I'm so sorry that you had to suffer with that horrible disease."

She tipped her head slightly to one side, as though to acknowledge what I had said about her suffering. Then she smiled—a beautiful smile—and said very distinctly, "But all I remember is love." And she disappeared.

I began to shiver in a room gone suddenly cold, and I knew in my bones that the love we give and receive is all that matters and is all that is remembered. Suffering disappears; love remains.

Her words are the most important I have ever heard, and that moment is forever engraved on my heart.

Bobbie Probstein

Memory is more indelible than ink.

Anita Loos

The Most Caring Child

Love is everything. It is the key to life, and its influences are those that move the world.

Ralph Waldo Trine

Author and lecturer Leo Buscaglia once talked about a contest he was asked to judge. The purpose of the contest was to find the most caring child. The winner was a four-year-old child whose next-door neighbor was an elderly gentleman who had recently lost his wife. Upon seeing the man cry, the little boy went into the old gentleman's yard, climbed onto his lap, and just sat there. When his mother asked him what he had said to the neighbor, the little boy said, "Nothing, I just helped him cry."

Ellen Kreidman

Compassion Is in the Eyes

It was a bitter, cold evening in northern Virginia many years ago. The old man's beard was glazed by winter's frost while he waited for a ride across the river. The wait seemed endless. His body became numb and stiff from the frigid north wind.

He heard the faint, steady rhythm of approaching hooves galloping along the frozen path. Anxiously, he watched as several horsemen rounded the bend. He let the first one pass by without an effort to get his attention. Then another passed by, and another. Finally, the last rider neared the spot where the old man sat like a snow statue. As this one drew near, the old man caught the rider's eye and said, "Sir, would you mind giving an old man a ride to the other side? There doesn't appear to be a passageway by foot."

Reigning his horse, the rider replied, "Sure thing. Hop aboard." Seeing the old man was unable to lift his half-frozen body from the ground, the horseman dismounted and helped the old man onto the horse. The horseman took the old man not just across the river, but to his destination, which was just a few miles away.

As they neared the tiny but cozy cottage, the horseman's curiosity caused him to inquire, "Sir, I notice that you let several other riders pass by without making an effort to secure a ride. Then I came up and you immediately asked me for a ride. I'm curious why, on such a bitter winter night, you would wait and ask the last rider. What if I had refused and left you there?"

The old man lowered himself slowly down from the horse, looked the rider straight in the eyes, and replied, "I've been around these here parts for some time. I reckon I know people pretty good." The old-timer continued, "I looked into the eyes of the other riders and immediately saw there was no concern for my situation. It would have been useless even to ask them for a ride. But when I looked into your eyes, kindness and compassion were evident. I knew, then and there, that your gentle spirit would welcome the opportunity to give me assistance in my time of need."

Those heartwarming comments touched the horseman deeply. "I'm most grateful for what you have said," he told the old man. "May I never get too busy in my own affairs that I fail to respond to the needs of others with kindness and compassion."

With that, Thomas Jefferson turned his horse around and made his way back to the White House.

Anonymous
From Brian Cavanaugh's The Sower's Seeds

*D*ignity and humility are the cornerstones of compassion.

Theodore Isaac Rubin

Whoever Finds This, I Love You!

On a quiet street in the city a little old man walked along
Shuffling through the autumn afternoon,
And the autumn leaves reminded him of other summers come
     and gone.
He had a long lonely night ahead waiting for June.

Then among the leaves near an orphans' home a piece of paper
     caught his eye,
And he stooped to pick it up with trembling hands.
As he read the childish writing the old man began to cry
'Cause the words burned inside him like a brand.

"Whoever finds this, I love you, whoever finds this, I need you
I ain't even got no one to talk to
So whoever finds this, I love you!"

The old man's eyes searched the orphans' home and came to rest
  upon a child
With her nose pressed up against the window pane.
And the old man knew he found a friend at last so he waved to her
  and smiled.
And they both knew they'd spend the winter laughing at the rain.
And they did spend the winter laughing at the rain
Talking through the fence and exchanging little gifts they had made
  for each other.

The old man would carve toys for the little girl.
She would draw pictures for him of beautiful ladies
Surrounded by green trees and sunshine, and they laughed a lot.
But then on the first day of June the little girl ran to the fence
To show the old man a picture she drew, but he wasn't there.
And somehow the little girl knew he wasn't coming back
So she went to her room, took a crayon and paper and wrote . . .

"Whoever finds this, I love you, whoever finds this, I need you
I ain't even got no one to talk to
So whoever finds this, I love you!"

Source Unknown

The Gift

Bennet Cerf relates this touching story about a bus that was bumping along a back road in the South.

In one seat a wispy old man sat holding a bunch of fresh flowers. Across the aisle was a young girl whose eyes came back again and again to the man's flowers. The time came for the old man to get off. Impulsively he thrust the flowers into the girl's lap. "I can see you love the flowers," he explained, "and I think my wife would like for you to have them. I'll tell her I gave them to you." The girl accepted the flowers, then watched the old man get off the bus and walk through the gate of a small cemetery.

Bennet Cerf

The Gentlest Need

At least once a day our old black cat comes to one of us in a way that we've all come to see as a special request. It does not mean he wants to be fed, or to be let out. His need is for something very different.

If you have a lap handy, he'll jump into it. Once in it, he begins to vibrate almost before you stroke his back, scratch his chin, and tell him over and over what a good kitty he is.

Our daughter puts it simply: "Blackie needs to be purred."

He isn't the only one who has that need: I share it, and so does my wife. Still, I associate it especially with youngsters, with their quick, impulsive need for a hug, a warm lap, and a hand held out.

If I could do just one thing, it would be this: To guarantee every child, everywhere, one good purring every day. Kids, like cats, need time to purr.

Fred T. Wilhelms

Two Brothers

For it is in giving that we receive.

Saint Francis of Assisi

Two brothers worked together on the family farm. One was married and had a large family. The other was single. At the day's end, the brothers shared everything equally, produce and profit.

Then one day the single brother said to himself, "It's not right that we should share equally the produce and the profit. I'm alone and my needs are simple." So each night he took a sack of grain from his bin and crept across the field between their houses, dumping it into his brother's bin.

Meanwhile, the married brother said to himself, "It's not right that we should share the produce and the profit equally. After all, I'm married and I have my wife and my children to look after me in years to come. My brother has no one, and no one to take care of his future." So each night he took a sack of grain and dumped it into his single brother's bin.

Both men were puzzled for years because their supply of grain never dwindled. Then one dark night the two brothers bumped into each other. Slowly it dawned on them what was happening. They dropped their sacks and embraced one another.

Source Unknown
From Brian Cavanaugh's More Sower's Seeds

Life in abundance comes only through great love.

Elbert Hubbard

Two Nickels and Five Pennies

When an ice cream sundae cost much less, a boy entered a coffee shop and sat at a table. A waitress put a glass of water in front of him. "How much is an ice cream sundae?"

"Fifty cents," replied the waitress.

The little boy pulled his hand out of his pocket and studied a number of coins in it. "How much is a dish of plain ice cream?" he inquired.

Some people were now waiting for a table, and the waitress was impatient. "Thirty-five cents," she said brusquely.

The little boy again counted the coins. "I'll have the plain ice cream."

The waitress brought the ice cream and walked away. The boy finished, paid the cashier, and departed. When the waitress came back, she swallowed hard at what she saw. There, placed neatly beside the empty dish, were two nickels and five pennies—her tip.

The Best of Bits & Pieces

2

LEARNING TO LOVE YOURSELF

Recognize Your Winners

The deepest principle in human nature is the craving to be appreciated.

William James

Fran Tarkenton, former Minnesota Vikings quarterback, once called a play that required him to block onrushing tacklers.

NFL quarterbacks almost never block. They're usually vastly outweighed by defenders, so blocking exposes them to the risk of severe injury.

But the team was behind, and a surprise play was needed. Tarkenton went in to block, and the runner scored a touchdown. The Vikings won the game.

Watching the game films with the team the next day, Tarkenton expected a big pat on the back for what he'd done.

It never came.

After the meeting, Tarkenton approached coach Bud Grant and asked, "You saw my block, didn't you, Coach? How come you didn't say anything about it?"

Grant replied, "Sure, I saw the block. It was great. But you're always working hard out there, Fran. I figured I didn't have to tell you."

"Well," Tarkenton replied, "if you ever want me to block again, you do!"

Don Martin

We increase whatever we praise. The whole creation responds to praise, and is glad.

Charles Fillmore

Be Yourself

You do not have to be your mother unless she is who you want to be. You do not have to be your mother's mother, or your mother's mother's mother, or even your grandmother's mother on your father's side. You may inherit their chins or their hips or their eyes, but you are not destined to become the women who came before you. You are not destined to live their lives. So if you inherit something, inherit their strength, their resilience. Because the only person you are destined to become is the person you decide to be.

Pam Finger

•   •   •   •   •

President Calvin Coolidge once invited friends from his hometown to dine at the White House. Worried about their table manners, the guests decided to do everything that Coolidge did. This strategy succeeded, until coffee was served. The president poured his coffee into the saucer. The guests did the same. Coolidge added sugar and cream. His guests did, too. Then Coolidge bent over and put his saucer on the floor for the cat.

Erik Oleson

I Like Myself Now

Once you see a child's self-image begin to improve, you will see significant gains in achievement areas, but even more important, you will see a child who is beginning to enjoy life more.

Wayne Dyer

I had a great feeling of relief when I began to understand that a youngster needs more than just subject matter. I know mathematics well, and I teach it well. I used to think that was all I needed to do. Now I teach children, not math. I accept the fact that I can only succeed partially with some of them. When I don't have to know all the answers, I seem to have more answers than when I tried to be the expert. The youngster who really made me understand this was Eddie. I asked him one day why he thought he was doing so much better than last year. He gave meaning to my whole new orientation. "It's because I like myself now when I'm with you," he said.

A teacher, quoted by Everett Shostrom
in Man, the Manipulator

What we sincerely believe regarding ourselves is true for us.
Orison Swett Marden

I am me and I am okay.
Virginia Satir

Ask for Appreciation

Everyone needs recognition for his accomplishments, but few people make the need known quite as clearly as the little boy who said to his father: "Lets play darts. I'll throw and you say 'Wonderful!'"

Bits & Pieces

If you treat an individual . . . as if he were what he ought to be and could be, he will become what he ought to be and could be.

Johann Wolfgang von Goethe

Covering All the Bases

A little boy was overheard talking to himself as he strode through his backyard, baseball cap in place and toting ball and bat. "I'm the greatest baseball player in the world," he said proudly. Then he tossed the ball in the air, swung and missed. Undaunted, he picked up the ball, threw it into the air and said to himself, "I'm the greatest baseball player ever!" He swung at the ball again, and again he missed. He paused a moment to examine the bat and ball carefully. Then once again he threw the ball into the air and said, "I'm the greatest baseball player who ever lived." He swung the bat hard and again missed the ball.

"Wow!" he exclaimed. "What a pitcher!"

Source Unknown

Start With Yourself

The following words were written on the tomb of an Anglican bishop in the crypts of Westminster Abbey:

When I was young and free and my imagination had no limits, I dreamed of changing the world. As I grew older and wiser, I discovered the world would not change, so I shortened my sights somewhat and decided to change only my country.

But it too seemed immovable.

As I grew into my twilight years, in one last desperate attempt, I settled for changing only family, those closest to me, but alas, they would have none of it.

And now as I lay on my deathbed, I suddenly realize: *If I had only changed my self first,* then by example I would have changed my family.

From their inspiration and encouragement, I would then have been able to better my country and, who knows, I may have even changed the world.

Anonymous

For of all sad words of tongue or pen, the saddest are these: "It might have been!"

John Greenleaf Whittier

Nothing but the Truth!

The truth simply is, that's all. It doesn't need reasons; it doesn't have to be right: it's just the truth. Period.

Carl Frederick

David Casstevens of the *Dallas Morning News* tells a story about Frank Szymanski, a Notre Dame center in the 1940s, who had been called as a witness in a civil suit at South Bend.

"Are you on the Notre Dame football team this year?" the judge asked.

"Yes, Your Honor."

"What position?"

"Center, Your Honor."

"How good a center?"

Szymanski squirmed in his seat, but said firmly: "Sir, I'm the best center Notre Dame has ever had."

Coach Frank Leahy, who was in the courtroom, was surprised. Szymanski always had been modest and unassuming. So when the proceedings were over, he took Szymanski aside and asked why he had made such a statement. Szymanski blushed.

"I hated to do it, Coach," he said. "But, after all, I *was* under oath."

David Casstevens

All necessary truth is its own evidence.

Ralph Waldo Emerson

You Are a Marvel

Each second we live is a new and unique moment of the universe that will never be again. . . . And what do we teach our children? That two and two make four, and that Paris is the capital of France.

We *should* say to each of them: Do you know what you are? You are a marvel. You are unique. In all the years that have passed, there has never been another child like you. Your legs, your arms, your clever fingers, the way you move.

You may become a Shakespeare, a Michelangelo, a Beethoven. You have the capacity for anything. Yes, you are a marvel. And when you grow up, can you then harm another who is, like you, a marvel?

We must all work to make the world worthy of its children.

Pablo Casals

Our Deepest Fear

Our deepest fear is not that we are inadequate.
Our deepest fear is that we are powerful beyond measure.
It is our Light, not our Darkness, that most frightens us.
We ask ourselves, who am I to be brilliant, gorgeous, talented, fabulous?
Actually, who are you NOT to be?
You are a child of God. Your playing small does not serve the World.
There is nothing enlightening about shrinking so that other people won't feel unsure around you.
We were born to make manifest the glory of God that is within us.
It is not just in some of us; it is in everyone.
As we let our own Light shine, we unconsciously give other people permission to do the same.
As we are liberated from our own fear, our presence automatically liberates others.

Marianne Williamson

$\overline{3}$

ON PARENTING

Tommy's Essay

Soon Tommy's parents, who had recently separated, would arrive for a conference on his failing schoolwork and disruptive behavior. Neither parent knew that I had summoned the other.

Tommy, an only child, had always been happy, cooperative, and an excellent student. How could I convince his father and mother that his recent failing grades represented a brokenhearted child's reaction to his adored parents' separation and pending divorce?

Tommy's mother entered and took one of the chairs I had placed near my desk. Then the father arrived. They pointedly ignored each other.

As I gave a detailed account of Tommy's behavior and schoolwork, I prayed for the right words to bring these two together to help them see what they were doing to their son. But somehow the words wouldn't come. Perhaps if they saw one of his smudged, carelessly done papers.

I found a crumpled, tear-stained sheet stuffed in the back of his desk. Writing covered both sides, a single sentence scribbled over and over.

Silently I smoothed it out and gave it to Tommy's mother. She read it and then without a word handed it to her husband. He frowned. Then his face softened. He studied the scrawled words for what seemed an eternity.

At last he folded the paper carefully and reached for his wife's outstretched hand. She wiped the tears from her eyes and smiled up at him. My own eyes were brimming, but neither seemed to notice.

In his own way God had given me the words to reunite that family. He had guided me to the sheet of yellow copy paper covered with the anguished outpouring of a small boy's troubled heart.

"Dear Mother . . . Dear Daddy . . . I love you . . . I love you . . . I love you."

Jane Lindstrom

Little Eyes Upon You

There are little eyes upon you
and they're watching night and day.
There are little ears that quickly
take in every word you say.
There are little hands all eager
to do anything you do;
and a little boy who's dreaming
of the day he'll be like you.

You're the little fellow's idol,
you're the wisest of the wise.
In his little mind about you
no suspicions ever rise.
He believes in you devoutly,
holds all you say and do;

He will say and do, in your way
when he's grown up like you.

There's a wide-eyed little fellow
who believes you're always right,
and his eyes are always opened,
and he watches day and night.
You are setting an example
every day in all you do,
to grow up to be like you.

Source Unknown
Submitted by Ronald Dahlsten

The Gift of the Gods

It was a warm summer day when the gods placed it in her hands. She trembled with emotion as she saw how fragile it appeared. This was a very special gift the gods were entrusting to her. A gift that would one day belong to the world. Until then, they instructed her, she was to be its guardian and protector. The woman said she understood and reverently took it home, determined to live up to the faith the gods had placed in her.

At first she barely let it out of her sight, protecting it from anything she perceived to be harmful to its well-being; watching with fear in her heart when it was exposed to the environment outside of the sheltered cocoon she had formed around it. But the woman began to realize that she could not shelter it forever. It needed to learn to survive the harsh elements in order to grow strong. So with gentle care she gave it more space to grow . . . enough to allow it to grow wild and untamed.

One day she became aware of how much the gift had changed. It no longer had a look of vulnerability about it. Now it seemed to glow with strength and steadiness, almost as if it were developing a power within. Month after month she watched as it became stronger and more powerful, and the woman remembered her promise. She knew deep within her heart that her time with the gift was nearing an end.

The inevitable day arrived when the gods came to take the gift and present it to the world. The woman felt a deep sadness, for she would miss its constant presence in her life. With heartfelt gratitude she thanked the gods for allowing her the privilege of watching over the precious gift for so many years. Straightening her shoulders, she stood proud, knowing that it was, indeed, a very special gift. One that would add to the beauty and essence of the world around it. And the mother let her child go.

Renee R. Vroman

But You Didn't

I looked at you and smiled the other day
I thought you'd see me but you didn't
I said "I love you" and waited for what you would say
I thought you'd hear me but you didn't
I asked you to come outside and play ball with me
I thought you'd follow me but you didn't
I drew a picture just for you to see
I thought you'd save it but you didn't
I made a fort for us back in the woods
I thought you'd camp with me but you didn't

I found some worms 'n' such for fishing if we could
I thought you'd want to go but you didn't
I needed you just to talk to, my thoughts to share
I thought you'd want to but you didn't

I told you about the game hoping you'd be there
I thought you'd surely come but you didn't
I asked you to share my youth with me
I thought you'd want to but you couldn't.
My country called me to war, you asked me to come home
safely.

But I didn't.

Stan Gebhardt

*D*eath *is a challenge. It tells us not to waste time. . . . It tells us
to tell each other right now that we love each other.*

Leo Buscaglia

What You Are Is as Important as What You Do

Honesty is the first chapter in the book of wisdom.

Thomas Jefferson

It was a sunny Saturday afternoon in Oklahoma City. My friend and proud father Bobby Lewis was taking his two little boys to play miniature golf. He walked up to the fellow at the ticket counter and said, "How much is it to get in?"

The young man replied, "$3.00 for you and $3.00 for any kid who is older than six. We let them in free if they are six or younger. How old are they?"

Bobby replied, "The lawyer's three and the doctor is seven, so I guess I owe you $6.00."

The man at the ticket counter said, "Hey, Mister, did you just win the lottery or something? You could have saved yourself three bucks. You could have told me that the older one was six; I wouldn't have known the difference." Bobby replied, "Yes, that may be true, but the kids would have known the difference."

As Ralph Waldo Emerson said, "Who you are speaks so loudly I can't hear what you're saying." In challenging times when ethics are more important than ever before, make sure you set a good example for everyone you work and live with.

Patricia Fripp

*N*o *legacy is so rich as honesty.*

William Shakespeare

Courage of the Heart

I sit on the rickety auditorium chair with the camcorder on my shoulder and I can feel the tears well up in my eyes. My six-year-old daughter is on stage, calm, self-possessed, centered and singing out her heart. I am nervous, jittery, emotional and trying not to cry.

"Listen, can you hear the sound, hearts beating all the world around?" she sings.

Little round face turned up to the light, little face so dear and familiar and yet so unlike my own thin features. Her eyes look out into the audience with total trust . . . she knows they love her. Eyes that don't look like mine.

"Up in the valley, out on the plains, everywhere around the world, heartbeats sound the same."

The face of her birth mother looks out at me from the stage. The eyes of a young woman that once looked into mine with trust now gaze into the audience. These features my daughter inherited from her birth mother . . . eyes that tilt up at the corners and rosy, plump little cheeks that I can't stop kissing.

"Black or white, red or tan, it's the heart of the family of man . . . oh, oh beating away, oh, oh beating away," she finishes.

The audience goes wild. I do, too. Thunderous applause, and they rise as one to let Melanie know they loved it. She smiles . . . she already knew. Now I am crying. I feel so blessed to be her mom . . . she fills me with so much joy that my heart actually hurts.

The heart of the family of man . . . the heart of courage that shows us the path to take when we are lost . . . the heart that makes strangers one with each other for a common purpose . . . this is the heart Melanie's birth mother showed to me. Melanie heard her from deep inside the safest part of her. This heart of courage belonged to a sixteen-year-old girl . . . a girl who became a woman because of her commitment to unconditional love. She was a woman who embraced the concept that she could give her child something no one else ever could . . . a better life than she had.

Melanie's heart beats close to mine as I hold her and tell her how great she performed. She wiggles in my arms and looks up at me. "Why are you crying, Mommie?"

I answer her, "Because I am so happy for you and you did so good, all by yourself!" I can feel myself reach out with tendrils of love and hold her with more than just my arms. I hold her with love for not only myself, but for the beautiful and courageous woman who chose to give birth to my daughter, and then chose again to give her to me. I carry the love from both of us . . . the birth mother with the courage to share, and the woman whose empty arms were filled with love . . . *for the heartbeat that we share is one.*

Patty Hansen

What It Means to Be Adopted

Teacher Debbie Moon's first graders were discussing a picture of a family. One little boy in the picture had different color hair than the other family members.

One child suggested that he was adopted and a little girl named Jocelynn Jay said, "I know all about adoptions because I'm adopted."

"What does it mean to be adopted?" asked another child.

"It means," said Jocelynn, "that you grew in your mother's heart instead of her tummy."

George Dolan

Legacy of an Adopted Child

Once there were two women who never knew each other.
One you do not remember, the other you call Mother.
Two different lives shaped to make you one.
One became your guiding star. The other became your sun.
The first one gave you life, the second taught you to live it.
The first gave you a need for love, the second was there to give it.
One gave you a nationality, the other gave you a name.
One gave you a talent, the other gave you aim.
One gave you emotions, the other calmed your fears.
One saw your first sweet smile, the other dried your tears.
One sought for you a home that she could not provide,
The other prayed for a child and her hope was not denied.
And now you ask me through your tears

The age-old question, unanswered through the years.
Heredity or environment. Which are you a product of?
Neither my darling. Neither. Just two different kinds of love.

Source Unknown

To an Adopted Child

Not flesh of my flesh, nor bone of my bone.
But still, miraculously, my own.
Never forget for a single minute,
You didn't grow under my heart
But in it.

Fleur Conklina Heulinger
Submitted by Jennifer Ann Kundert

He Is Just a Little Boy

He stands at the plate
with his heart pounding fast.
The bases are loaded,
the die has been cast.
Mom and Dad cannot help him,
he stands all alone.
A hit at this moment,
would send the team home.
The ball meets the plate,
he swings and he misses.
There's a groan from the crowd,
with some boos and some hisses.
A thoughtless voice cries,
"Strike out the bum."

Tears fill his eyes,
the game's no longer fun.
So open your heart and give him a break,
For it's moments like this,
a man you can make.
Please keep this in mind,
when you hear someone forget.
He is just a little boy, and not a man yet.

Chaplain Bob Fox

My Father When I Was . . .

4 years old: My daddy can do anything.

5 years old: My daddy knows a whole lot.

6 years old: My dad is smarter than your dad.

8 years old: My dad doesn't know exactly everything.

10 years old: In the olden days when my dad grew up, things were sure different.

12 years old: Oh, well, naturally, Father doesn't know anything about that. He is too old to remember his childhood.

14 years old: Don't pay any attention to my father. He is so old-fashioned!

21 years old: Him? My Lord, he's hopelessly out-of-date.

25 years old: Dad knows a little bit about it, but then he should because he has been around so long.

30 years old: Maybe we should ask Dad what he thinks. After all, he's had a lot of experience.

35 years old: I'm not doing a single thing until I talk to Dad.

40 years old: I wonder how Dad would have handled it. He was so wise and had a world of experience.

50 years old: I'd give anything if Dad were here now so I could talk this over with him. Too bad I didn't appreciate how smart he was. I could have learned a lot from him.

Ann Landers

A place is nothing, not even space, unless at its heart a figure stands.

Amy Lowell

Paco Come Home

In a small town in Spain, a man named Jorge had a bitter argument with his young son Paco. The next day Jorge discovered that Paco's bed was empty—he had run away from home.

Overcome with remorse, Jorge searched his soul and realized that his son was more important to him than anything else. He wanted to start over. Jorge went to a well-known store in the center of town and posted a large sign that read, "Paco, come home. I love you. Meet me here tomorrow morning."

The next morning Jorge went to the store, where he found no less than seven young boys named Paco who had also run away from home. They were all answering the call for love, hoping it was their father inviting them home with open arms.

Alan Cohen

If I Had My Child to Raise Over Again

If I had my child to raise all over again,
I'd finger-paint more, and point the finger less.
I would do less correcting and more connecting.
I'd take my eyes off my watch, and watch with my eyes.
I would care to know less and know to care more.
I'd take more hikes and fly more kites.
I'd stop playing serious, and seriously play.
I would run through more fields and gaze at more stars.
I'd do more hugging and less tugging.
I'd build self-esteem first, and the house later.
I would be firm less often, and affirm much more.
I'd teach less about the love of power,
And more about the power of love.

Diane Loomans
from the book, Full Esteem Ahead, 100 Ways to Build Self-Esteem in Children and Adults

Rescued

A little girl whose parents had died lived with her grandmother and slept in an upstairs bedroom.

One night there was a fire in the house and the grandmother perished while trying to rescue the child. The fire spread quickly, and the first floor of the house was soon engulfed in flames.

Neighbors called the fire department, then stood helplessly by, unable to enter the house because flames blocked all the entrances. The little girl appeared at an upstairs window, crying for help, just as word spread among the crowd that firefighters would be delayed a few minutes because they were all at another fire.

Suddenly, a man appeared with a ladder, put it up against the side of the house and disappeared inside. When he reappeared, he had the little girl in his arms. He delivered the child to the waiting arms below, then disappeared into the night.

An investigation revealed that the child had no living relatives, and weeks later a meeting was held in the town hall to determine who would take the child into their home and bring her up.

A teacher said she would like to raise the child. She pointed out that she could ensure her a good education. A farmer offered her an upbringing on his farm. He pointed out that living on a farm was healthy and satisfying. Others spoke, giving their reasons why it was to the child's advantage to live with them.

Finally, the town's richest resident arose and said, "I can give this child all the advantages that you have mentioned here, plus money and everything that money can buy."

Throughout all this, the child remained silent, her eyes on the floor.

"Does anyone else want to speak?" asked the meeting chairman. A man came forward from the back of the hall. His gait was slow and he seemed in pain. When he got to the front of the room, he stood directly before the little girl and held out his arms. The crowd gasped. His hand and arms were terribly scarred.

The child cried out, "This is the man who rescued me!" With a leap, she threw her arms around the man's neck, holding on for dear life, just as she had that fateful night. She buried her face on his shoulder and sobbed for a few moments. Then she looked up and smiled at him.

"This meeting is adjourned," said the chairman.

from *Leadership . . . with a human touch*

*N*ot he who has much is rich, but he who gives much.

Erich Fromm

Barney

A four-year-old girl was at the pediatrician for a check up. As the doctor looked down her ears with an otoscope, he asked, "Do you think I'll find Big Bird in here?" The little girl stayed silent.

Next, the doctor took a tongue depressor and looked down her throat. He asked, "Do you think I'll find the Cookie Monster down there?" Again, the little girl was silent.

Then the doctor put a stethoscope to her chest. As he listened to her heart beat, he asked, "Do you think I'll hear Barney in here?"

"Oh, no!" the little girl replied. "Jesus is in my heart. Barney's on my underpants."

Source Unknown

No Charge

Our little boy came up to his mother and handed her a piece of paper. After his mom dried her hands on an apron, she read it:

For cutting the grass.	$5.00
For cleaning up my room this week.	$1.00
For going to the store for you.	.50
Baby-sitting my kid brother.	.25
Taking out the garbage.	$1.00
For getting a good report card.	$5.00
For cleaning up, and raking the yard.	$2.00
Total owed:	$14.75

His mother looked at him standing there, expectantly. She picked up the pen, turned the paper over and wrote:

Nine months I carried you while you were inside me: No Charge.

The times I've sat with you, doctored and prayed for you: No Charge.

For all the tears that you've caused through the years: No Charge.

For all the nights that were filled with dread, and the worries I knew were ahead: No Charge.

For the toys, food, clothes, and even wiping your nose, there's No Charge, son.

And when you add it all up, the full cost of real love is, No Charge.

When our son finished reading what his mother had written, there were great big old tears in his eyes. He looked straight at his mother and said, "Mom, I sure do love you." And then he took the pen and in great big letters he wrote: "PAID IN FULL."

M. Adams

Almie Rose

It was at least two months before Christmas when nine-year-old Almie Rose told her father and me that she wanted a new bicycle. As Christmas drew nearer, her desire for a bicycle seemed to fade, or so we thought. We purchased the latest rage, Baby-Sitter's Club dolls, and a doll house. Then, much to our surprise, on December 23rd, she said that she "really wanted a bike more than anything else."

It was just too late, what with all the details of preparing Christmas dinner and buying last-minute gifts, to take the time to select the "right bike" for our little girl. So, here we were—Christmas Eve around 9:00 P.M., with Almie Rose and her six-year-old brother, Dylan, nestled snug in their beds. We could now think only of the bicycle, the guilt, and being parents who would disappoint their child.

"What if I make a little bicycle out of clay and write a note that she could trade the clay model in for a real bike?" her dad asked. The theory being that since this is a high-ticket item and she is "such a big girl," it would be much better for her to pick it out. So he spent the next four hours painstakingly working with clay to create a miniature bike.

On Christmas morning, we were excited for Almie Rose to open the little heart-shaped package with the beautiful red and white clay bike and the note. Finally, she opened it and read the note aloud.

"Does this mean that I trade in this bike that Daddy made me for a real one?" Beaming, I said, "Yes."

Almie Rose had tears in her eyes when she replied, "I could never trade in this beautiful bicycle that Daddy made me. I'd rather keep this than get a real bike."

At that moment, we would have moved heaven and earth to buy her every bicycle on the planet!

Michelle Lawrence

"If you're raisin' me right,
HOW COME I GET INTO SO MUCH TROUBLE?"

DENNIS THE MENACE® used by permission of Hank Ketcham and © by North America Syndicate.

4

ON TEACHING
AND LEARNING

The Rules for Being Human

1. **You will receive a body.**
   You may like it or hate it, but it will be yours for the entire period.
2. **You will learn lessons.**
   You are enrolled in a full-time informal school called Life. Each day in this school you will learn lessons. You may like the lessons or think them irrelevant and stupid.
3. **There are no mistakes, only lessons.**
   Growth is a process of trial and error: experimentation. The "failed" experiments are as much a part of the process as the experiment that ultimately "works."
4. **A lesson is repeated until learned.**
   A lesson will be presented to you in various forms until you have learned it. Once learned, you then go on to the next lesson.

5. **Learning lessons does not end.**
   There is no part of life that does not contain its lessons. If you are alive, there are lessons to be learned.

6. **"There" is no better than "here."**
   When your "there" has become a "here," you will simply obtain another "there" that will again look better than "here."

7. **Others are merely mirrors of you.**
   You cannot love or hate something about another person unless it reflects something you love or hate about yourself.

8. **What you make of your life is up to you.**
   You have all the tools and resources you need. What you do with them is up to you. The choice is yours.

9. **The answers to Life's questions lie inside you.**
   All you need to do is look, listen and trust.

10. **You will forget all this.**

Chérie Carter-Scott

A Sense of a Goose

When you see geese flying along in "V" formation, you might consider what science has discovered as to why they fly that way. As each bird flaps its wings, it creates an uplift for the bird immediately following. By flying in "V" formation, the whole flock adds at least 71 percent greater flying range than if each bird flew on its own.

People who share a common direction and sense of community can get where they are going more quickly and easily because they are traveling on the thrust of one another.

When a goose falls out of formation, it suddenly feels the drag and resistance of trying to go it alone—and quickly gets back into formation to take advantage of the lifting power of the bird in front.

If we have as much sense as a goose, we will stay in formation with those people who are headed the same way we are.

When the head goose gets tired, it rotates back in the wing and another goose flies point.

It is sensible to take turns doing demanding jobs, whether with people or with geese flying south.

Geese honk from behind to encourage those up front to keep up their speed.

What messages do we give when we honk from behind?

Finally—and this is important—when a goose gets sick or is wounded by gunshot, and falls out of formation, two other geese fall out with that goose and follow it down to lend help and protection. They stay with the fallen goose until it is able to fly or until it dies; and only then do they launch out on their own, or with another formation to catch up with their group.

If we have the sense of a goose, we will stand by each other like that.

Source Unknown

Adam

To have character is to be big enough to take life on.

Mary Caroline Richards

While recuperating from her second open-heart surgery at Children's Hospital of Western Ontario, my six-year-old daughter, Kelley, was moved from the intensive care unit to the floor with the other children. Because a section of the floor was closed, Kelley was put in the wing reserved for cancer patients.

In the adjacent room, a six-year-old boy named Adam was fighting a battle with leukemia. Adam stayed at the hospital for a portion of each month while receiving chemotherapy treatments. Every day Adam sauntered into Kelley's room to visit, pushing the pole that held his chemotherapy bag. Despite the discomfort of the treatments, Adam was always smiling and cheerful. He entertained us for hours with his many stories. Adam had a way of finding the positive and the humor in any situation, however difficult.

One particular day, I was feeling tired and anxious for Kelley's release from the hospital. The gray, gloomy day outside only fueled my poor mood. While I stood at the window looking at the rainy sky, Adam came in for his daily visit. I commented to him on what a depressing day it was. With his ever-present smile, Adam turned to me and cheerily replied, "Every day is beautiful for me."

From that day on I have never had a gloomy day. Even the grayest days bring a feeling of joy as I remember with gratitude the words of wisdom spoken by a very brave six-year-old boy named Adam.

Patti Merritt

The Hand

When you give yourself, you receive more than you give.

Antoine de Saint Exupéry

A Thanksgiving Day editorial in the newspaper told of a school teacher who asked her class of first-graders to draw a picture of something they were thankful for. She thought of how little these children from poor neighborhoods actually had to be thankful for. But she knew that most of them would draw pictures of turkeys or tables with food. The teacher was taken aback with the picture Douglas handed in . . . a simple childishly drawn hand.

But whose hand? The class was captivated by the abstract image. "I think it must be the hand of God that brings us food," said one child. "A farmer," said another, "because he grows the turkeys." Finally when the others were at work, the teacher bent over Douglas' desk and asked whose hand it was. "It's your hand, Teacher," he mumbled.

She recalled that frequently at recess she had taken Douglas, a scrubby forlorn child, by the hand. She often did that with the children. But it meant so much to Douglas. Perhaps this was everyone's Thanksgiving, not for the material things given to us but for the chance, in whatever small way, to give to others.

Source Unknown

In helping others, we shall help ourselves, for whatever good we give out completes the circle and comes back to us.

Flora Edwards

If I Had My Life to Live Over

I'd dare to make more mistakes next time.

I'd relax. I would limber up.

I would be sillier than I have been this trip.

I would take fewer things seriously.

I would take more chances.

I would take more trips.

I would climb more mountains and swim more rivers.

I would eat more ice cream and less beans.

I would perhaps have more actual troubles but I'd have fewer imaginary ones.

You see, I'm one of those people who live sensibly and sanely hour after hour, day after day.

Oh, I've had my moments and if I had it to do over again, I'd have more of them. In fact, I'd try to have nothing else. Just moments.

One after another, instead of living so many years ahead of each day.

I've been one of those people who never go anywhere without a thermometer, a hot water bottle, a raincoat and a parachute.
If I had it to do again, I would travel lighter next time.

If I had my life to live over, I would start barefoot earlier in the spring and stay that way later in the fall.
I would go to more dances.
I would ride more merry-go-rounds.
I would pick more daisies.

Nadine Stair (age 85)

Golden Rules for Living

Consideration for others is the basis of a good life, a good society.

Confucious

If you open it, close it.
If you turn it on, turn it off.
If you unlock it, lock it up.
If you break it, admit it.
If you can't fix it, call in someone who can.
If you borrow it, return it.
If you value it, take care of it.
If you make a mess, clean it up.
If you move it, put it back.
If it belongs to someone else and you want to use it, get permission.
If you don't know how to operate it, leave it alone.

If it's none of your business, don't ask questions.
If it ain't broke, don't fix it.
If it will brighten someone's day, say it.
If it will tarnish someone's reputation, keep it to yourself.

Source Unknown

As human beings, we are endowed with freedom of choice, and we cannot shuffle off our responsibility upon the shoulders of God or nature. We must shoulder it ourselves. It is up to us.

Arnold J. Toynbee

The Secrets of Heaven and Hell

The old monk sat by the side of the road. With his eyes closed and his legs crossed and his hands folded in his lap, he sat. In deep meditation, he sat.

Suddenly his *zazen* was interrupted by the harsh and demanding voice of a samurai warrior. "Old man! Teach me about Heaven and Hell!"

At first, as though he had not heard, there was no perceptible response from the monk. But gradually, he began to open his eyes, the faintest hint of a smile playing around the corners of his mouth as the samurai stood there waiting . . . impatient . . . growing more and more agitated with each passing second.

"You would know the secrets of Heaven and Hell?" replied the monk at last. "You who are so unkempt. You whose hands and feet are covered with dirt. You whose hair is uncombed, whose breath is foul, whose sword is all rusty and neglected. You who are ugly and whose mother dresses you funny. You would ask me of Heaven and Hell?"

The samurai uttered a vile curse. He drew his sword and raised it high above his head. His face turned to crimson, the veins on his neck stood out in bold relief as he prepared to sever the monk's head from its shoulders.

"That is Hell," said the old monk gently, just as the sword began its descent.

In that fraction of a second, the samurai was overcome with amazement, awe, compassion and love for this gentle being who had dared to risk his very life to give him such a teaching. He stopped his sword in mid-flight and his eyes filled with grateful tears.

"And that," said the monk, "is Heaven."

Father John W. Groff Jr.

It's Never Too Late

Each experience through which we pass operates for our good.
. . . This is a correct attitude to adopt . . . and we must be able
to see it in that light.

Raymond Holliwell

Several years ago, while attending a communications course, I experienced a most unusual process. The instructor asked us to list anything in our past that we felt ashamed of, guilty about, regretted, or incomplete about. The next week he invited participants to read their lists aloud. This seemed like a very private process, but there's always some brave soul in the crowd who will volunteer. As people read their lists, mine grew longer. After three weeks, I had 101 items on my list. The instructor then suggested that we find ways to make amends, apologize to people, or take some action to right any wrongdoing. I was seriously wondering how this could ever improve my communications, having visions of alienating just about everyone from my life.

The next week, the man next to me raised his hand and volunteered this story:

"While making my list, I remembered an incident from high school. I grew up in a small town in Iowa. There was a sheriff in town that none of us kids liked. One night, my two buddies and I decided to play a trick on Sheriff Brown. After drinking a few beers, we found a can of red paint, climbed the tall water tank in the middle of town, and wrote, on the tank, in bright red letters: Sheriff Brown is an s.o.b. The next day, the town arose to see our glorious sign. Within two hours, Sheriff Brown had my two pals and me in his office. My friends confessed and I lied, denying the truth. No one ever found out.

"Nearly 20 years later, Sheriff Brown's name appears on my list. I didn't even know if he was still alive. Last weekend, I dialed information in my hometown back in Iowa. Sure enough, there was a Roger Brown still listed. I dialed his number. After a few rings, I heard: 'Hello?' I said: 'Sheriff Brown?' Pause. 'Yup.' 'Well, this is Jimmy

Calkins. And I want you to know that I did it.' Pause. 'I knew it!' he yelled back. We had a good laugh and a lively discussion. His closing words were: 'Jimmy, I always felt badly for you because your buddies got it off their chest, and I knew you were carrying it around all these years. I want to thank you for calling me . . . *for your sake*.'"

Jimmy inspired me to clear up all 101 items on my list. It took me almost two years, but became the springboard and true inspiration for my career as a conflict mediator. No matter how difficult the conflict, crisis or situation, I always remember that it's never too late to clear up the past and begin resolution.

Marilyn Manning

5
ON DEATH
AND DYING

On Death

Do not stand at my grave and weep.
I am not there.
I do not sleep.
I am a thousand winds that blow.
I am the diamond glint on snow.
I am the sunlight on ripened grain.
I am the autumn rain.
When you awake in the morning hush,
I am the swift uplifting rush
Of birds circling in flight.
I am the stars that shine at night.
Do not stand at my grave and weep.
I am not there.
I do not sleep.

Source Unknown

Death is simply a shedding of the physical body, like the butterfly coming out of a cocoon. It is a transition into a higher state of consciousness, where you continue to perceive, to understand, to laugh, to be able to grow, and the only thing you lose is something that you don't need anymore . . . your physical body. It's like putting away your winter coat when spring comes.

Elisabeth Kübler-Ross

The Prettiest Angel

The heart of a fool is in his mouth, but the mouth of a wise man is in his heart.

Benjamin Franklin

For the past 20 years I have spoken to all kinds of audiences in the character of Benjamin Franklin, complete with costume. One day after a school assembly, I was visiting a fifth-grade classroom to answer questions. One student raised his hand and said, "I thought you died." This was not an unusual question and I answered it by saying, "Well, I did die on April 17, 1790, when I was 84 years old, but I didn't like it and I'm never going to do it again."

I immediately asked for any other questions and called on a boy at the back of the room who raised his hand. He asked, "When you were in Heaven, did you see my mother there?"

My heart stopped. I wanted the floor to open up and swallow me.

My only thought was, don't blow this! I realized for an 11-year-old boy to ask that question in front of all of his classmates, it had to either be a very recent occurrence or of utmost concern. I also knew I had to say something.

Then I heard my voice say: "I'm not sure if she is the one I think she was, but if she is, she was the prettiest angel there."

The smile on his face told me that it was the right answer. I'm not sure where it came from, but I think I just may have had a little help from the prettiest angel there.

Ralph Archbold

To Remember Me

The day will come when my body will lie upon a white sheet neatly tucked under four corners of a mattress located in a hospital busily occupied with the living and the dying. At a certain moment a doctor will determine that my brain has ceased to function and that, for all intents and purposes, my life has stopped.

When that happens, do not attempt to instill artificial life into my body by the use of a machine. And don't call this my deathbed. Let it be called the Bed of Life, and let my body be taken from it to help others lead fuller lives.

Give my sight to the man who has never seen a sunrise, a baby's face or love in the eyes of a woman. Give my heart to a person whose own heart has caused nothing but endless days of pain. Give my blood to the teenager who was pulled from the wreckage of his car, so that he might live to see his grandchildren play. Give my kidneys to one who depends on a machine to exist from week to week. Take my bones, every muscle, every fiber and nerve in my body and find a way to make a crippled child walk.

Explore every corner of my brain. Take my cells, if necessary, and let them grow so that, someday, a speechless boy will shout at the crack of a bat and a deaf girl will hear the sound of rain against her window.

Burn what is left of me and scatter the ashes to the winds to help the flowers grow.

If you must bury something, let it be my faults, my weaknesses and all prejudice against my fellow man.

Give my sins to the devil. Give my soul to God.

If, by chance, you wish to remember me, do it with a kind deed or word to someone who needs you. If you do all I have asked, I will live forever.

Robert N. Test

Please Dress Me in Red

In my profession, I have worked with children who have the virus that causes AIDS. The relationships that I have had with these special kids have been gifts in my life. Let me tell you about the courage of Tyler.

Tyler was born infected with HIV; his mother was also infected. From the very beginning of his life, he was dependent on medications to enable him to survive. At times, he also needed supplemental oxygen to support his breathing.

Tyler wasn't willing to give up one single moment of his childhood to this deadly disease. It was not unusual to find him playing and racing around his backyard, wearing his medicine-laden backpack and dragging his tank of oxygen behind him in his little wagon. Tyler's pure joy in being alive gave him energy that caused all of us who knew him to marvel. Tyler's mom often teased him by telling him that he moved so fast, she needed to dress him in red. That way, when she peered out the window to check on him playing in the yard, she could quickly spot him.

This dreaded disease eventually wore down even the likes of a little dynamo like Tyler. He became quite ill and, unfortunately, so did his mother. When it became apparent that he wasn't going to survive, Tyler's mom talked to him and she comforted him by telling Tyler that she was dying, too, and that she would be with him soon in heaven.

A few days before his death, Tyler beckoned me over to his hospital bed and whispered, "I might die soon. I'm not scared. When I die, please dress me in red. Mom promised she's coming to heaven, too. I'll be playing when she gets there, and I want to make sure she can find me."

Cindy Dee Holms

The Eternal Optimist

We have been lucky to be blessed with three sons. Our middle son, Billy, is fondly known as "the eternal optimist." For example, he had always been an early riser and liked to get in our bed at 5 A.M. We would admonish him to be quiet and go back to sleep. He would say in a falsetto whisper, "It's going to be a beautiful morning. I hear the birds singing." When we would ask him to stop talking, he would reply, "I not talking to you; I talking to me!"

In kindergarten, he was asked to draw a tiger. Art is not his strong suit, and his tiger came out with one eye that appeared to be shut. When asked why the tiger had one eye closed, he replied, "Because he's saying, 'Here's looking at you, kid!'"

Once he got into an argument with his older brother about whether a man on TV was bald. Billy said, "He's not bald. He's only bald when he looks at you. When he walks away, he has lots of hair!"

These memories and many more led up to the ultimate optimistic statement. Our third son was stricken with hemolytic uremic syndrome on a Tuesday and died on the following Sunday. The night after Tanner's funeral, I had laid down beside Billy to discuss the day, as we often did. On this night, we were lying in the dark with not much to say. Suddenly, Billy spoke. "I feel sorry for us, but I almost feel more sorry for all those other people." Which people was he talking about? "The people who never knew Tanner. Weren't we lucky to have had Tanner with us for 20 months. Just think, there are lots of people who were never lucky enough to know him at all. We are really lucky people."

Beth Dalton

MISTER BOFFO by Joe Martin

©1995 Joe Martin, Inc./Dist. by Universal Press Syndicate

6

A MATTER OF ATTITUDE

The Optimist

The optimist sees the doughnut, the pessimist, the hole.

McLandburgh Wilson

There is a story of identical twins. One was a hope-filled optimist. "Everything is coming up roses!" he would say. The other twin was a sad and hopeless pessimist. He thought that Murphy, as in Murphy's Law, was an optimist. The worried parents of the boys brought them to the local psychologist.

He suggested to the parents a plan to balance the twins' personalities. "On their next birthday, put them in separate rooms to open their gifts. Give the pessimist the best toys you can afford, and give the optimist a box of manure." The parents followed these instructions and carefully observed the results.

When they peeked in on the pessimist, they heard him audibly complaining, "I don't like the color of this computer . . . I'll bet this calculator will break . . . I don't like the game . . . I know someone who's got a bigger toy car than this . . ."

Tiptoeing across the corridor, the parents peeked in and saw their little optimist gleefully throwing the manure up in the air. He was giggling. "You can't fool me! Where there's this much manure, there's gotta be a pony!"

Source Unknown
From Brian Cavanaugh's More Sower's Seeds

Whiners

When my grandmother was raising me in Stamps, Arkansas, she had a particular routine when people who were known to be whiners entered her store. My grandmother would ask the customer, "How are you doing today, Brother Thomas?"

And the person would reply, "Not so good today, Sister Henderson. You see, it's this summer heat. I just hate it. It just frazzles me up and frazzles me down. It's almost killing me." Then my grandmother would stand stoically, her arms folded, and mumble, "Uh-huh, uh-huh." And she would cut her eyes at me to make certain that I had heard the lamentation.

As soon as the complainer was out of the store, my grandmother would call me to stand in front of her. And then she would say the same thing she had said at least a thousand times, it seemed to me. "Sister, did you hear what Brother So-and-So or Sister Much-to-Do complained about?" And I would nod. Mamma would continue,

"Sister, there are people who went to sleep all over the world last night, poor and rich and white and black, but they will never wake again. And those dead folks would give anything, anything at all for just five minutes of this weather that person was grumbling about. So you watch yourself about complaining, Sister. What you're supposed to do when you don't like a thing is change it. If you can't change it, change the way you think about it. Don't complain."

It is said that persons have few teachable moments in their lives. Mamma seemed to have caught me at each one I had. Whining is not only graceless, but can be dangerous. It can alert a brute that a victim is in the neighborhood.

Maya Angelou

Good News

Two men look out through the same bars: One sees the mud, and one the stars.

Frederick Langbridge

Robert De Vincenzo, the great Argentine golfer, once won a tournament and, after receiving the check and smiling for the cameras, he went to the clubhouse and prepared to leave. Some time later, he walked alone to his car in the parking lot and was approached by a young woman. She congratulated him on his victory and then told him that her child was seriously ill and near death. She did not know how she could pay the doctor's bills and hospital expenses.

De Vincenzo was touched by her story, and he took out a pen and endorsed his winning check for payment to the woman. "Make some good days for the baby," he said as he pressed the check into her hand.

The next week he was having lunch in a country club when a

Professional Golf Association official came to his table. "Some of the boys in the parking lot last week told me you met a young woman there after you won that tournament." De Vincenzo nodded. "Well," said the official, "I have news for you. She's a phony. She has no sick baby. She's not even married. She fleeced you, my friend."

"You mean there is no baby who is dying?" said De Vincenzo.

"That's right," said the official.

"That's the best news I've heard all week," De Vincenzo said.

The Best of Bits & Pieces

Great Value in Disaster

If your house is on fire, warm yourself by it.

Spanish Proverb

Thomas Edison's laboratory was virtually destroyed by fire in December, 1914. Although the damage exceeded two million dollars, the buildings were only insured for $238,000 because they were made of concrete and thought to be fireproof. Much of Edison's life's work went up in spectacular flames that December night.

At the height of the fire, Edison's 24-year-old son, Charles, frantically searched for his father among the smoke and debris. He finally found him, calmly watching the scene, his face glowing in the reflection, his white hair blowing in the wind.

"My heart ached for him," said Charles. "He was 67—no longer a young man—and everything was going up in flames. When he saw me, he shouted, 'Charles, where's your mother?' When I told him I didn't know, he said, 'Find her. Bring her here. She will never see anything like this as long as she lives.'"

The next morning, Edison looked at the ruins and said, "There is great value in disaster. All our mistakes are burned up. Thank God we can start anew."

Three weeks after the fire, Edison managed to deliver his first phonograph.

From Brian Cavanaugh's The Sower's Seeds

A Place to Stand

If you have ever gone through a toll booth, you know that your relationship to the person in the booth is not the most intimate you'll ever have. It is one of life's frequent nonencounters: You hand over some money; you might get change; you drive off.

Late one morning in 1984, headed for lunch in San Francisco, I drove toward a booth. I heard loud music. It sounded like a party. I looked around. No other cars with their windows open. No sound trucks. I looked at the toll booth. Inside it, the man was dancing.

"What are you doing?" I asked.

"I'm having a party," he said.

"What about the rest of the people?" I looked at the other toll booths.

He said, "What do those look like to you?" He pointed down the row of toll booths.

"They look like . . . toll booths. What do they look like to you?"

He said, "Vertical coffins. At 8:30 every morning, live people get in.

Then they die for eight hours. At 4:30, like Lazarus from the dead, they reemerge and go home. For eight hours, brain is on hold, dead on the job. Going through the motions."

I was amazed. This guy had developed a philosophy, a mythology about his job. Sixteen people dead on the job, and the seventeenth, in precisely the same situation, figures out a way to *live*. I could not help asking the next question: "Why is it different for you? You're having a good time."

He looked at me. "I knew you were going to ask that. I don't understand why anybody would think my job is boring. I have a corner office, glass on all sides. I can see the Golden Gate, San Francisco, and the Berkeley hills. Half the Western world vacations here . . . and I just stroll in every day and practice dancing."

Dr. Charles Garfield

When We're Alone, We Can Dance

The cruise ship was crowded with people off for three days of pleasure. Ahead of me in the passageway walked a tiny woman in brown slacks, her shoulders hunched, her white hair cut in a bob.

From the ship's intercom came a familiar tune—"Begin the Beguine." And suddenly, a wonderful thing happened. The woman, unaware anyone was behind her, did a quick and graceful dance step—back, shuffle, slide.

As she reached the door to the dining salon, she re-assembled her dignity, and stepped soberly through.

Younger people often think folks my age are beyond romance, dancing or dreams. They see us as age has shaped us; camouflaged by wrinkles, thick waists and gray hair.

They don't see the people who live inside—we are the wise old codgers, the dignified matrons.

No one would ever know that I am still the skinny girl who grew up in a leafy suburb of Boston. Inside, I still think of myself as the youngest child in a vivacious family headed by a mother of great beauty and a father of unfailing good cheer.

And I am still the romantic teenager who longed for love, the young adult who aspired to social respectability—but whom shall I tell?

We are all like the woman in the ship's passageway, in whom the music still echoes. We are the sum of all the lives we once lived. We show the grown-up part, but inside we are still the laughing children, the shy teens, the dream-filled youths. There still exists, most real, the matrix of all we were or ever yearned to be.

In our hearts we still hear "Begin the Beguine"—and when we are alone, we dance.

Beth Ashley

The Cookie Thief

A woman was waiting at an airport one night,
With several long hours before her flight.
She hunted for a book in the airport shop,
Bought a bag of cookies and found a place to drop.

She was engrossed in her book, but happened to see
That the man beside her, as bold as could be,
Grabbed a cookie or two from the bag between,
Which she tried to ignore, to avoid a scene.

She read, munched cookies and watched the clock,
As the gutsy "cookie thief" diminished her stock.
She was getting more irritated as the minutes ticked by,
Thinking, "If I wasn't so nice, I'd blacken his eye!"

With each cookie she took, he took one, too.
When only one was left, she wondered what he'd do.
With a smile on his face and a nervous laugh,
He took the last cookie and broke it in half.

He offered her half, as he ate the other.
She snatched it from him and thought, "Oh brother,
This guy has some nerve, and he's also *rude*.
Why, he didn't even show any gratitude!"

She had never known when she had been so galled,
And sighed with relief when her flight was called.
She gathered her belongings and headed for the gate,
Refusing to look back at the "thieving ingrate."

She boarded the plane and sank in her seat,
Then sought her book, which was almost complete.
As she reached in her baggage, she gasped with surprise.
There was her bag of cookies in front of her eyes!

"If mine are here," she moaned with despair,
"Then the others were *his* and he tried to share!"
Too late to apologize, she realized with grief
That *she* was the rude one, the ingrate, the thief!

Valerie Cox

Do unto others as you would have them do unto you.

Matt. 7:12

Discouraged?

As I was driving home from work one day, I stopped to watch a local Little League baseball game that was being played in a park near my home. As I sat down behind the bench on the first-baseline, I asked one of the boys what the score was.

"We're behind 14 to nothing," he answered with a smile.

"Really," I said. "I have to say you don't look very discouraged."

"Discouraged?" the boy asked with a puzzled look on his face. "Why should we be discouraged? We haven't been up to bat yet."

Jack Canfield

Lady, Are You Rich?

They huddled inside the storm door—two children in ragged outgrown coats.

"Any old papers, lady?"

I was busy. I wanted to say no—until I looked down at their feet. Thin little sandals, sopped with sleet. "Come in and I'll make you a cup of hot cocoa." There was no conversation. Their soggy sandals left marks upon the hearthstone.

Cocoa and toast with jam to fortify against the chill outside. I went back to the kitchen and started again on my household budget . . .

The silence in the front room struck through to me. I looked in.

The girl held the empty cup in her hands, looking at it. The boy asked in a flat voice, "Lady . . . are you rich?"

"Am I rich? Mercy, no!" I looked at my shabby slipcovers.

The girl put her cup back in its saucer—carefully. "Your cups match your saucers." Her voice was old with a hunger that was not of the stomach.

They left then, holding their bundles of papers against the wind. They hadn't said thank you. They didn't need to. They had done more than that. Plain blue pottery cups and saucers. But they matched. I tested the potatoes and stirred the gravy. Potatoes and brown gravy—a roof over our heads—my man with a good steady job—these things matched, too.

I moved the chairs back from the fire and tidied the living room. The muddy prints of small sandals were still wet upon my hearth. I let them be. I want them there in case I ever forget again how very rich I am.

Marion Doolan

Class Reunion

It's amazing how a phone call can totally turn one's life upside down. It had been a former high school classmate asking for help with our 20-year reunion.

Had it been 20 years already?

I shuddered. Cold chills went up and down my spine as tiny beads of sweat popped out on my forehead. What had I done with my life in the past 20 years?

I glanced in the mirror. I examined every tiny crevice, starting with my hairline, down past those patronizing "smile lines" to the base of my neck. No double chin yet, I thought.

The next few weeks were pure hell. Each day began with a 6:30 A.M. run in a futile attempt to bounce off the unsightly baggage that had somehow accumulated on my thighs overnight. I went shopping for the perfect dress—you know, the one that would make me look 20 years younger. Three dress shops later, I came to my senses. There was only one logical explanation: I was having a mid-life crisis.

I realized that the funny, crunching noise I heard each night as I climbed the stairs was really my knees. Bran flakes had become a part of my daily routine—and not because they were my favorite cereal.

Life just hadn't turned out the way I'd planned. Sure, I was happy. I had a wonderful husband and two great kids. But somehow, working part-time as a secretary and mom hardly fit my definition of someone my classmates had voted as "most likely to succeed." Had I really wasted 20 years?

About the time I was ready to throw in the towel, my seven-year-old tapped me on the shoulder. "I love you, Mom. Give me a kiss."

You know, I'm actually looking forward to the next 20 years.

Lynne C. Gaul

Roles—and How We Play Them

Whenever I'm disappointed with my spot in life, I stop and think about little Jamie Scott. Jamie was trying out for a part in a school play. His mother told me that he'd set his heart on being in it, though she feared he would not be chosen. On the day the parts were awarded, I went with her to collect him after school. Jamie rushed up to her, eyes shining with pride and excitement. "Guess what, Mum," he shouted, and then said those words that remain a lesson to me: "I've been chosen to clap and cheer."

Marie Curling

7

OVERCOMING
OBSTACLES

The Miracle Bridge

The Brooklyn Bridge that spans the river between Manhattan and Brooklyn is simply an engineering miracle. In 1883, a creative engineer, John Roebling, was inspired by an idea for this spectacular bridge project. However, bridge-building experts told him to forget it, it just was not possible. Roebling convinced his son, Washington, an up-and-coming engineer, that the bridge could be built. The two of them conceived the concept of how it could be accomplished, and how to overcome the obstacles. Somehow they convinced bankers to finance the project. Now with unharnessed excitement and energy, they hired their crew and began to build their dream bridge.

The project was only a few months under way when a tragic on-site accident killed John Roebling and severely injured his son. Washington was severely brain-damaged, unable to talk or walk. Everyone thought that the project would have been scrapped since the Roeblings were the only ones who understood how the bridge could be built.

Though Washington Roebling was unable to move or talk, his mind was as sharp as ever. One day, as he lay in his hospital bed, an idea flashed in his mind as to how to develop a communication code. All he could move was one finger, so he touched the arm of his wife with that finger. He tapped out the code to communicate to her what she was to tell the engineers who continued building the bridge. For 13 years, Washington tapped out his instructions with one finger until the spectacular Brooklyn Bridge was finally completed.

From Brian Cavanaugh's A Fresh Packet of Sower's Seeds

A Lesson in Heart

A lesson in "heart" is my little, 10-year-old daughter, Sarah, who was born with a muscle missing in her foot and wears a brace all the time. She came home one beautiful spring day to tell me she had competed in "field day"—that's where they have lots of races and other competitive events.

Because of her leg support, my mind raced as I tried to think of encouragement for my Sarah, things I could say to her about not letting this get her down—but before I could get a word out, she said, "Daddy, I won two of the races!"

I couldn't believe it! And then Sarah said, "I had an advantage."

Ahh. I knew it. I thought she must have been given a head start . . . some kind of physical advantage. But again, before I could say anything, she said, "Daddy, I didn't get a head start . . . my advantage was I had to try harder!"

That's heart! That's my Sarah.

Stan Frager

Obstacles

We who lived in the concentration camps can remember the men who walked through the huts comforting others, giving away their last piece of bread. They may have been few in number, but they offer sufficient proof that everything can be taken from a man but one thing: The last of his freedoms—to choose one's attitude in any given set of circumstances, to choose one's own way.

Viktor E. Frankl
Man's Search for Meaning

The greatest power that a person possesses is the power to choose.

J. Martin Kohe

Faith

Down in the reception room of the Institute of Physical Medicine and Rehabilitation, there's a bronze plaque that's riveted to the wall. During the months I went to the Institute for treatment, I rolled through that reception room many times, coming and going. But I never quite made the time to pull over to one side and read the words on that plaque that were written, it's said, by an unknown Confederate soldier. Then one afternoon, I did. I read it and then I read it again. When I finished it for the second time I was near to bursting—not in despair, but with an inner glow that had me straining to grip the arms of my wheelchair. I'd like to share it with you:

A Creed for Those Who Have Suffered

I asked God for strength, that I might achieve.
I was made weak, that I might learn humbly to obey . . .

I asked for health, that I might do great things.
I was given infirmity, that I might do better things . . .
I asked for riches, that I might be happy.
I was given poverty, that I might be wise . . .
I asked for power, that I might have the praise of men.
I was given weakness, that I might feel the need of God . . .
I asked for all things, that I might enjoy life.
I was given life, that I might enjoy all things . . .
I got nothing I asked for—but everything I had hoped for.
Almost despite myself, my unspoken prayers were answered.
I am, among men, most richly blessed!

Roy Campanella

Don't Be Afraid to Fail

You've failed many times, although you may not remember.
You fell down the first time you tried to walk.
You almost drowned the first time you tried to swim, didn't you?
Did you hit the ball the first time you swung a bat?
Heavy hitters, the ones who hit the most home runs, also strike out a lot.
R.H. Macy failed seven times before his store in New York caught on.
English novelist John Creasey got 753 rejection slips before he published 564 books.
Babe Ruth struck out 1330 times, but he also hit 714 home runs.
Don't worry about failure.
Worry about the chances you miss when you don't *even try.*

Wall Street Journal

What's Really Important

A few years ago at the Seattle Special Olympics, nine contestants, all physically or mentally disabled, assembled at the starting line for the 100-yard dash. At the gun they all started out, not exactly in a dash, but with the relish to run the race to the finish and win.

All, that is, except one boy who stumbled on the asphalt, tumbled over a couple of times, and began to cry. The other eight heard the boy cry. They slowed down and paused. Then they all turned around and went back. Every one of them. One girl with Down's syndrome bent down and kissed him and said, "This will make it better." Then all nine linked arms and walked together to the finish line.

Everyone in the stadium stood and the cheering went on for ten minutes.

Bob French

Consider This

- General Douglas MacArthur was turned down for admission to West Point not once but twice. But he tried a third time, was accepted and marched into the history books.
- Basketball superstar Michael Jordan was cut from his high school basketball team.
- In 1889, Rudyard Kipling received the following rejection letter from the *San Francisco Examiner:* "I'm sorry, Mr. Kipling, but you just don't know how to use the English language."
- Winston Churchill failed sixth grade. He did not become Prime Minister of England until he was 62, and then only after a lifetime of defeats and setbacks. His greatest contributions came when he was a "senior citizen."
- The parents of the famous opera singer Enrico Caruso wanted him to be an engineer. His teacher said he had no voice at all and could not sing.

- Albert Einstein did not speak until he was four years old and didn't read until he was seven. His teacher described him as "mentally slow, unsociable and adrift forever in his foolish dreams." He was expelled and was refused admittance to the Zurich Polytechnic School.
- Louis Pasteur was only a mediocre pupil in undergraduate studies and ranked 15th out of 22 in chemistry.
- In 1944, Emmeline Snively, director of the Blue Book Modeling Agency, told modeling hopeful Norma Jean Baker (Marilyn Monroe), "You'd better learn secretarial work or else get married."
- While turning down the British rock group called the Beatles, one executive of Decca Recording Company said, "We don't like their sound. Groups of guitars are on the way out."
- In 1954, Jimmy Denny, manager of the Grand Ole Opry, fired Elvis Presley after one performance. He told Presley, "You ain't goin' nowhere . . . son. You ought to go back to drivin' a truck."

- When Alexander Graham Bell invented the telephone in 1876, it did not ring off the hook with calls from potential backers. President Rutherford Hayes said, "That's an amazing invention, but who would ever want to use one of them?"
- Rafer Johnson, the decathlon champion, was born with a club foot.
- When Thomas Edison invented the light bulb, he tried over 2,000 experiments before he got it to work. A young reporter asked him how it felt to fail so many times. He said, "I never failed once. I invented the light bulb. It just happened to be a 2,000-step process."
- After years of progressive hearing loss, by age 46 German composer Ludwig van Beethoven had become completely deaf. Nevertheless, he wrote his greatest music—including five symphonies—during his later years.

Jack Canfield and Mark Victor Hansen

The Beauty Remains; The Pain Passes

Although Henri Matisse was nearly twenty-eight years younger than Auguste Renoir, the two great artists were dear friends and frequent companions. When Renoir was confined to his home during the last decade of his life, Matisse visited him daily. Renoir, almost paralyzed by arthritis, continued to paint in spite of his infirmities. One day, as Matisse watched the elder painter working in his studio, fighting tortuous pain with each brush stroke, he blurted out: "Auguste, why do you continue to paint when you are in such agony?" Renoir answered simply: "The beauty remains; the pain passes." And so, almost to his dying day, Renoir put paint to canvas. One of his most famous paintings, *The Bathers,* was completed just two years before his passing, fourteen years after he was stricken by this disabling disease.

The Best of Bits & Pieces

We Never Told Him He Couldn't Do It

My son Joey was born with club feet. The doctors assured us that with treatment he would be able to walk normally—but would never run very well. The first three years of his life were spent in surgery, casts and braces. By the time he was eight, you wouldn't know he had a problem when you saw him walk.

The children in our neighborhood ran around as most children do during play, and Joey would jump right in and run and play, too. We never told him that he probably wouldn't be able to run as well as the other children. So he didn't know.

In seventh grade he decided to go out for the cross-country team. Every day he trained with the team. He worked harder and ran more than any of the others—perhaps he sensed that the abilities that seemed to come naturally to so many others did not come naturally to him. Although the entire team runs, only the top seven runners have the potential to score points for the school. We didn't tell him he probably would never make the team, so he didn't know.

He continued to run four to five miles a day, every day—even the day he had a 103-degree fever. I was worried, so I went to look for him after school. I found him running all alone. I asked him how he felt. "Okay," he said. He had two more miles to go. The sweat ran down his face and his eyes were glassy from his fever. Yet he looked straight ahead and kept running. We never told him he couldn't run four miles with a 103-degree fever. So he didn't know.

Two weeks later, the names of the team runners were called. Joey was number six on the list. Joey had made the team. He was in seventh grade—the other six team members were all eighth-graders. We never told him he shouldn't expect to make the team. We never told him he couldn't do it. We never told him he couldn't do it . . . so he didn't know. He just did it.

Kathy Lamancusa

The Passionate Pursuit of Possibility

Cherish your visions and your dreams as they are the children of your soul; the blueprints of your ultimate achievements.

Napoleon Hill

Years ago, while unearthing an ancient Egyptian tomb, an archaeologist came upon seeds buried in a piece of wood. Planted, the seeds realized their potential after more than 3,000 years! Are there conditions in the lives of people so discouraging, so defeating, that human beings—regardless of inherent potentiality—are doomed to lives of failure and quiet desperation? Or are there also seeds of possibility in people, an urge for becoming that is so strong, that the hard crust of adversity is breached? Consider this story that came over the wires of the Associated Press on May 23, 1984:

As a child, Mary Groda did not learn to read and write. Experts labeled her retarded. As an adolescent she "earned" an additional label, "incorrigible," and was sentenced to two years in a reformatory. It was here, ironically, in this closed-in place, that Mary—bending to the challenge to learn—worked at her task for as long as 16 hours a day. Her hard work paid off. She was awarded her (GED) high school diploma.

But more misfortune was to visit Mary Groda. After leaving the reformatory, she became pregnant without benefit of marriage. Then, two years later a second pregnancy resulted in a stroke, erasing her hard-earned powers of reading and writing. With the help and support of her father, Mary battled back, regaining what she had lost.

In dire financial straits, Mary went on welfare. Finally, to make ends meet, she took in seven foster children. It was during this period that she started taking courses at a community college. Upon completion of her course work, she applied to and was accepted by the Albany Medical School to study medicine.

In the spring of 1984 in Oregon, Mary Groda Lewis—she's married now—paraded in full academic regalia across the graduation stage. No one can know what private thoughts went through Mary's mind as she

reached out to grasp this eloquent testimony to her self-belief and per-
severance, her diploma that announced to all the world: Here stands
on this small point of planet Earth a person who dared to dream the
impossible dream, a person who confirms for all of us our human
divineness. Here stands Mary Groda Lewis, MD.

James E. Conner

*Your chances of success in any undertaking can always be
measured by your belief in yourself.*

Robert Collier

Are You Strong Enough to Handle Critics?

It is not the critic who counts, not the man who points out how the strong man stumbles or where the doer of deeds could have done them better. The credit belongs to the man who is actually in the arena, whose face is marred by dust and sweat and blood, who strives valiantly, who errs and comes short again and again because there is no effort without error and shortcomings, who knows the great devotion, who spends himself in a worthy cause, who at his best knows in the end the high achievement of triumph and who at worst, if he fails while daring greatly, knows his place shall never be with those timid and cold souls who know neither victory nor defeat.

Theodore Roosevelt

Just One More Time

There's a 19th-century English novel in which every year for the past 500 years the people all gather in church on Christmas Eve and pray. Shortly before midnight they light candle lanterns and, singing carols and hymns, they walk several miles to an old abandoned stone shack. There they set up a manger scene. And in simple piety, they kneel and pray.

There is a myth in that town, a belief that if all citizens are present on Christmas Eve, and if all are praying with perfect faith, then and only then, the Second Coming will be at hand. For 500 years they've come to that stone ruin and prayed. Yet the Second Coming has eluded them.

One of the main characters in this novel is asked, "Do you believe that He will come again on Christmas Eve in our town?"

"No," he answers, shaking his head sadly. "No, I don't."

"Then why do you go each year?" he is asked.

"Ah," he says smiling, "what if I were the only one that wasn't there when it happened?"

As it says in the New Testament, we need only have faith as small as a grain of mustard seed to get into the Kingdom of Heaven. Sometimes, when we work with disturbed children, at-risk youth, troubled teens, alcoholic, abusive or depressed and suicidal partners or friends, we need that small bit of faith—the same that kept that man coming back. Just one more time. Just this next time, perhaps the breakthrough will come.

We sometimes are called upon to work with people for whom others have abandoned all hope. Perhaps even we have come to the conclusion that there's no possibility of change or growth. It's at that time that, if we can find the tiniest scrap of hope, we may turn the corner, achieve a measurable gain, save someone worth saving. Please go back, my friend, just this one more time.

Hanoch McCarty, Ed.D.

Cartoon by Ted Goff.

8

LIVE YOUR DREAM

Let There Be Peace

A wise old gentleman retired and purchased a modest home near a junior high school. He spent the first few weeks of his retirement in peace and contentment. . . . then a new school year began. The very next afternoon three young boys, full of youthful, after-school enthusiasm, came down his street, beating merrily on every trash can they encountered. The crashing percussion continued day after day, until finally the wise old man decided it was time to take some action.

The next afternoon, he walked out to meet the young percussionists as they banged their way down the street. Stopping them, he said, "You kids are a lot of fun. I like to see you express your exuberance like that. Used to do the same thing when I was your age. Will you do me a favor? I'll give you each a dollar if you'll promise to come around every day and do your thing."

The kids were elated and continued to do a bang-up job on the trash cans. After a few days, the old-timer greeted the kids again, but this time he had a sad smile on his face. "This recession's really putting a big dent in my income," he told them. "From now on, I'll only be able to pay you 50 cents to beat on the cans." The noisemakers were obviously displeased, but they did accept his offer and continued their afternoon ruckus.

A few days later, the wily retiree approached them again as they drummed their way down the street. "Look," he said, "I haven't received my Social Security check yet, so I'm not going to be able to give you more than 25 cents. Will that be okay?"

"A lousy quarter?" the drum leader exclaimed. "If you think we're going to waste our time, beating these cans around for a quarter, you're nuts! No way, mister. We quit!" And the old man enjoyed peace and serenity for the rest of his days.

Gentle Spaces News

Not a One!

Little Chad was a shy, quiet, young man. One day he came home and told his mother that he'd like to make a valentine for everyone in his class. Her heart sank. She thought, "I wish he wouldn't do that!" because she had watched the children when they walked home from school. They laughed and hung on to each other and talked to each other. But Chad was never included. Nevertheless, she decided she would go along with her son. So she purchased the paper and glue and crayons. Night after night, Chad painstakingly made 35 valentines.

Valentine's Day dawned, and Chad was beside himself with excitement. He carefully stacked them up, put them in a bag, and bolted out the door. His mother decided to bake him his favorite cookies and serve them nice and warm with a cool glass of milk when he came home from school. She just knew he would be disappointed, and maybe that would ease the pain a little. It hurt her to think that he wouldn't get many valentines—maybe none at all.

That afternoon she had the cookies and milk on the table. When she heard the children outside, she looked out the window. Sure enough there they came, laughing and having the best time. And, as always, there was Chad in the rear. He walked a little faster than usual. She fully expected him to burst into tears as soon as he got inside. His arms were empty, she noticed, and when the door opened she choked back the tears.

"Mommy has some cookies and milk for you," she said.

But he hardly heard her words. He just marched right on by, his face aglow, and all he could say was: "Not a one. Not a one."

Her heart sank.

And then he added, "I didn't forget a one, not a single one!"

Dave Galloway

One at a Time

To try is all. It matters not if one succeeds or fails outwardly.

Robert Thibodeau

A friend of ours was walking down a deserted Mexican beach at sunset. As he walked along, he began to see another man in the distance. As he grew nearer, he noticed that the local native kept leaning down, picking something up and throwing it out into the water. Time and again he kept hurling things out into the ocean.

As our friend approached even closer, he noticed that the man was picking up starfish that had been washed up on the beach and, one at a time, he was throwing them back into the water.

Our friend was puzzled. He approached the man and said, "Good evening, friend. I was wondering what you are doing."

"I'm throwing these starfish back into the ocean. You see, it's low tide right now and all of these starfish have been washed up onto the shore. If I don't throw them back into the sea, they'll die up here from lack of oxygen."

"I understand," my friend replied, "but there must be thousands of starfish on this beach. You can't possibly get to all of them. There are simply too many. And don't you realize this is probably happening on hundreds of beaches all up and down this coast? Can't you see that you can't possibly make a difference?"

The local native smiled, bent down and picked up yet another starfish, and as he threw it back into the sea, he replied, "Made a difference to that one!"

Jack Canfield and Mark Victor Hansen

Service with a Smile

If you could choose one characteristic that would get you through life, choose a sense of humor.

Jennifer James

A man wrote a letter to a small hotel in a Midwest town he planned to visit on his vacation. He wrote:

I would very much like to bring my dog with me. He is well-groomed and very well behaved. Would you be willing to permit me to keep him in my room with me at night?

An immediate reply came from the hotel owner, who said,

I've been operating this hotel for many years. In all that time, I've never had a dog steal towels, bedclothes or silverware or pictures off the walls.

I've never had to evict a dog in the middle of the night for being drunk and disorderly. And I've never had a dog run out on a hotel bill.

Yes, indeed, your dog is welcome at my hotel. And, if your dog will vouch for you, you're welcome to stay here, too.

Karl Albrecht and Ron Zenke
Service America

Near this spot are deposited the remains of one who possessed beauty without vanity, strength without insolence, courage without ferocity, and all the virtues of Man, without his vices. This praise, which would be unmeaning flattery if inscribed over human ashes, is but a just tribute to the memory of Boatswain, a dog.

Lord Byron

Encouragement

It takes so little to make people happy. Just a touch, if we know how to give it, just a word fitly spoken . . . a slight readjustment of some bolt or pin or bearing in the delicate machinery of a soul.

Frank Crane

Some of the greatest success stories of history have followed a word of encouragement or an act of confidence by a loved one or a trusting friend. Had it not been for a confident wife, Sophia, we might not have listed among the great names of literature the name of Nathaniel Hawthorne. When Nathaniel, a heartbroken man, went home to tell his wife that he was a failure and had been fired from his job in a customhouse, she surprised him with an exclamation of joy.

"Now," she said triumphantly, "you can write your book!"

"Yes," replied the man, with sagging confidence, "and what shall we live on while I am writing it?"

To his amazement, she opened a drawer and pulled out a substantial amount of money.

"Where on earth did you get that?" he exclaimed.

"I have always known that you were a man of genius," she told him. "I knew that someday you would write a masterpiece. So every week, out of the money you gave me for housekeeping, I saved a little bit. So here is enough to last us for one whole year."

From her trust and confidence came one of the greatest novels of American literature, *The Scarlet Letter*.

Nido Qubein

Did the Earth Move for You?

Eleven-year-old Angela was stricken with a debilitating disease involving her nervous system. She was unable to walk, and the doctors did not hold out much hope of her ever recovering. The little girl was undaunted. There, lying in her hospital bed, she would vow to anyone who'd listen that she was definitely going to be walking again someday.

She was transferred to a specialized rehabilitation hospital in the San Francisco Bay area. The therapists were charmed by her undefeatable spirit. They taught her about *imaging*—about seeing herself walking. If it would do nothing else, it would at least give her hope and something positive to do in the long waking hours in her bed. Angela would work as hard as possible in physical therapy, in whirlpools and in exercise sessions. But she worked just as hard lying there faithfully doing her imaging, visualizing herself moving, moving, moving!

One day, as she was straining with all her might to imagine her legs moving again, it seemed as though a miracle happened: The bed moved! It began to move around the room! She screamed out, "Look what I'm doing! Look! Look! I can do it! I moved, I *moved!*"

Of course, at this very moment everyone else in the hospital was screaming, too, and running for cover. People were screaming, equipment was falling, and glass was breaking. You see, it was an earthquake. But don't tell that to Angela. She's convinced that she did it. And now, only a few years later, she's back in school. On her own two legs. No crutches, no wheelchair. You see, anyone who can shake the earth between San Francisco and Oakland can conquer a piddling little disease, can't they?

Hanoch McCarty, Ed.D.

Risking

It is when we all play safe that we create a world of utmost insecurity.

Dag Hammarskjöld

Two seeds lay side by side in the fertile spring soil.

The first seed said, "I want to grow! I want to send my roots deep into the soil beneath me, and thrust my sprouts through the earth's crust above me . . . I want to unfurl my tender buds like banners to announce the arrival of spring . . . I want to feel the warmth of the sun on my face and the blessing of the morning dew on my petals!"

And so she grew.

The second seed said, "I am afraid. If I send my roots into the ground below, I don't know what I will encounter in the dark. If I push my way through the hard soil above me I may damage my delicate sprouts . . . what if I let my buds open and a snail tries to eat them? And if I were to open my blossoms, a small child may pull me from the ground. No, it is much better for me to wait until it is safe."

And so she waited.

A yard hen scratching around in the early spring ground for food found the waiting seed and promptly ate it.

> *Moral of the story:*
> *Those of us who refuse*
> *to risk and grow*
> *get swallowed up by life.*

Patty Hansen

Try Something Different

I'm sitting in a quiet room, in a peaceful little hotel hidden back among the pine trees. It's just past noon, late July, and I am listening to the desperate sounds of a life-or-death struggle going on a few feet away.

There's a small fly burning out the last of its short life's energies in a futile attempt to fly through the glass of the windowpane. The whining wings tell the poignant story of the fly's strategy: *Try harder.*

But it's not working.

The frenzied effort offers no hope for survival. Ironically, the struggle is part of the trap. It is impossible for the fly to try hard enough to succeed at breaking through the glass. Nevertheless, this little insect has staked its life on reaching its goal through raw effort and determination.

This fly is doomed. It will die there on the windowsill.

Ten steps away, the door is open. Ten seconds of flying time and this small creature could reach the outside world it seeks. With only a fraction of the effort now being wasted, it could be free of this self-imposed trap. The breakthrough possibility is there. It would be so easy.

Why doesn't the fly try another approach, something dramatically different? How did it get so locked in on the idea that this particular route and determined effort offer the most promise for success? What logic is there in continuing, until death, to seek a breakthrough with more of the same?

No doubt this approach makes sense to the fly. Regrettably, it's an idea that will kill.

Trying harder isn't necessarily the solution to achieving more. It may not offer any real promise for getting what you want out of life. Sometimes, in fact, it's a big part of the problem.

If you stake your hopes for a breakthrough on trying harder than ever, you may kill your chances for success.

Price Pritchett

The Magic of Believing

I'm not old enough to play baseball or football. I'm not eight yet. My mom told me when you start baseball, you aren't going to be able to run that fast because you had an operation. I told Mom I wouldn't need to run that fast. When I play baseball, I'll just hit them out of the park. Then I'll be able to walk.

Edward J. McGrath Jr.
"An Exceptional View of Life"

This is where you will win the battle—in the playhouse of your mind.

Maxwell Maltz

9

ECLECTIC
WISDOM

An Afternoon in the Park

There once was a little boy who wanted to meet God. He knew it was a long trip to where God lived, so he packed his suitcase with Twinkies and a six-pack of root beer and he started his journey.

When he had gone about three blocks, he met an old woman. She was sitting in the park just staring at some pigeons. The boy sat down next to her and opened his suitcase. He was about to take a drink from his root beer when he noticed that the old lady looked hungry, so he offered her a Twinkie. She gratefully accepted it and smiled at him. Her smile was so pretty that the boy wanted to see it again, so he offered her a root beer. Once again she smiled at him. The boy was delighted!

They sat there all afternoon eating and smiling, but they never said a word.

As it began to grow dark, the boy realized how tired he was and he got up to leave. He turned around, ran back to the old woman and gave her a hug. She gave him her biggest smile ever.

When the boy opened the door to his own house a short time later, his mother was surprised by the look of joy on his face.

She asked him, "What did you do today that made you so happy?"

He replied, "I had lunch with God. You know what? She's got the most beautiful smile I've ever seen!"

Meanwhile, the old woman, also radiant with joy, returned to her home.

Her son was stunned by the look of peace on her face and he asked, "Mother, what did you do today that made you so happy?"

She replied, "I ate Twinkies in the park with God. You know, he's much younger than I expected."

Julie A. Manhan

Two Monks

Two monks on a pilgrimage came to the ford of a river. There they saw a girl dressed in all her finery, obviously not knowing what to do since the river was high and she did not want to spoil her clothes. Without more ado, one of the monks took her on his back, carried her across and put her down on dry ground on the other side.

Then the monks continued on their way. But the other monk after an hour started complaining, "Surely it is not right to touch a woman; it is against the commandments to have close contact with women. How could you go against the rules for monks?"

The monk who had carried the girl walked along silently, but finally he remarked, "I set her down by the river an hour ago, why are you still carrying her?"

Irmgard Schloegl
The Wisdom of Zen Masters

Shoes

As Gandhi stepped aboard a train one day, one of his shoes slipped off and landed on the track. He was unable to retrieve it as the train was moving. To the amazement of his companions, Gandhi calmly took off his other shoe and threw it back along the track to land close to the first. Asked by a fellow passenger why he did so, Gandhi smiled. "The poor man who finds the shoe lying on the track," he replied, "will now have a pair he can use."

Source Unknown
First quoted in The Little, Brown Book of Anecdotes

God's Jobs

Danny Sutton, eight years old, wrote this for his third-grade Sunday School teacher, who asked her students to explain God:

One of God's main jobs is making people. He makes these to put in the place of the ones who die so there will be enough people to take care of things here on earth. He doesn't make grownups, he just makes babies. I think because they are smaller and easier to make. That way he doesn't have to take up his valuable time teaching them to walk and talk. He can just leave that up to the mothers and fathers. I think it works out pretty good.

God's second most important job is listening to prayers. An awful lot of this goes on, 'cause some people, like preachers and things, pray other times besides bedtimes, and Grandpa and Grandma pray every time they eat, except for snacks. God doesn't have time to listen to the radio or watch TV on account of this. 'Cause God hears everything, there must be a terrible lot of noise in his ears unless he has thought of a way to turn it down.

God sees and hears everything and is everywhere, which keeps him pretty busy. So you shouldn't go wasting his time asking for things that aren't important, or go over parents' heads and ask for something they said you couldn't have. It doesn't work anyway.

Dan Sutton
Christ Church
St. Michael's, Maryland
Submitted by Vanessa Hewko

What Goes Around Comes Around

When I was working as a disc jockey in Columbus, Ohio, I used to stop at a local hospital on my way home. I would walk into different people's rooms and read Scripture to them or talk to them. It was a way of forgetting about my problems and being thankful to God. It made a difference in the lives of those I visited. One time it literally saved my life.

One night I came home at about two o'clock in the morning. As I began to open my door, a man came out from behind the side of my house and said, "Are you Les Brown?"

I said, "Yes, sir."

He said, "I was sent here to carry out a contract on you."

"Me? Why?" I asked.

He said, "Well, there's a promoter that's very upset about the money you cost him when you said that the entertainers who were coming to town were not the original real group."

"Are you going to do something to me?" I asked.

He said, "No—I'll tell you why. My mother was in Grant Hospital and she wrote me about how you came in one day and sat down and talked to her and read Scripture to her. She was so impressed that this morning disc jockey, who didn't know her, came in and did that. She wrote me about you when I was in the Ohio penitentiary. I was impressed with that and I've always wanted to meet you. When I heard the word out on the street that somebody wanted to knock you off," he said, "I accepted the contract and then told them to leave you alone."

Les Brown

Angel with a Red Hat

I was scared as I sat in the coffee shop. Tomorrow I would have spinal surgery. The risk was high, but my faith was strong. I prayed, "Oh, heavenly Father, in my time of trial, send me an angel."

As I looked up, preparing to leave, I saw an elderly lady walking very slowly to the register. I stood by her, admiring her flair for fashion—a bright paisley dress of red and purple, a scarf, a brooch, and a brilliant scarlet hat. I said, "Excuse me, madam. I just must say what a beautiful woman you are."

She clasped my hand and said, "My child, bless you, for you see, I have an artificial arm and a plate in the other, and my leg is not my own. It takes me quite some time to get dressed. I do my best, but as years go by, people don't seem to think it matters. You've made me feel so special today. May the Lord watch over and bless you." As she walked away, she had touched my soul in such a way that I knew she could have only been the angel.

Tami S. Fox

A Small Boy

A small boy looked at a star
And began to weep.
And the star said,
Boy why are you weeping?
And the boy said,
You are so far away
I will never be able to touch you.
And the star answered,
Boy if I were not already in your heart
You would not be able to see me.

John Magliola

The Secret of Life

Life is a succession of lessons which must be lived to be understood.

Ralph Waldo Emerson

As the Lord God was creating the world
he called upon his archangels.
The Lord asked his archangels to help
him decide where to put the Secret of Life.

"Bury it in the ground," one angel replied.
"Put it on the bottom of the sea," said another.
"Hide it in the mountains," another suggested.

The Lord replied, "If I see to do any of those
only a few will find the Secret of Life.

The Secret of Life must be accessible to
EVERYONE!"

One angel replied, "I know, put it in each
man's heart,
Nobody will think to look there."
"Yes!" said the Lord. "Within each man's heart."
And so it was—
The SECRET OF LIFE lies within all of us.

Source Unknown

The Station

Tucked away in our subconscious is an idyllic vision. We are traveling by train—out the windows, we drink in the passing scenes of children waving at a crossing, cattle grazing on a distant hillside, row upon row of corn and wheat, flatlands and valleys, mountains and rolling hillsides and city skylines.

But uppermost in our minds is the final destination. On a certain day, we will pull into the station. Bands will be playing and flags waving. Once we get there, our dreams will come true and the pieces of our lives will fit together like a completed jigsaw puzzle. Restlessly we pace the aisles, damning the minutes—waiting, waiting, waiting for the station.

"When we reach the station, that will be it!" we cry. "When I'm 18." "When I buy a new 450SL Mercedes Benz!" "When I put the last kid through college." "When I have paid off the mortgage!" "When I get a promotion." "When I reach retirement, I shall live happily ever after!"

Sooner or later, we realize there is no station, no one place to arrive. The true joy of life is the trip. The station is only a dream. It constantly outdistances us.

"Relish the moment" is a good motto, especially when coupled with Psalm 118:24: "This is the day which the Lord hath made; we will rejoice and be glad in it." It isn't the burdens of today that drive men mad. It is the regrets over yesterday and the fear of tomorrow. Regret and fear are twin thieves who rob us of today.

So stop pacing the aisles and counting the miles. Instead, climb more mountains, eat more ice cream, go barefoot more often, swim more rivers, watch more sunsets, laugh more, cry less. Life must be lived as we go along. The station will come soon enough.

Robert J. Hastings

Footprints

One night I dreamed a dream.
I was walking along the beach with my Lord.
Across the dark sky flashed scenes from my life.
For each scene, I noticed two sets
of footprints in the sand,
one belonging to me
and one to my Lord.
When the last scene of my life shot before me
I looked back at the footprints in the sand.
There was only one set of footprints.
I realized that this was at the lowest
and saddest times of my life.
This always bothered me
and I questioned the Lord
about my dilemma.

"Lord, you told me when I decided to follow You,
You would walk and talk with me all the way.
But I'm aware that during the most troublesome
times of my life there is only one set of footprints.
I just don't understand why, when I needed You most,
You leave me."
He whispered, "My precious child,
I love you and will never leave you
never, ever, during your trials and testings.
When you saw only one set of footprints
it was then that I carried you."

Margaret Fishback Powers

Sachi

Soon after her brother was born, little Sachi began to ask her parents to leave her alone with the new baby. They worried that like most four-year-olds, she might feel jealous and want to hit or shake him, so they said no. But she showed no signs of jealousy. She treated the baby with kindness, and her pleas to be left alone with him became more urgent. They decided to allow it.

Elated, she went into the baby's room and shut the door, but it opened a crack—enough for her curious parents to peek in and listen. They saw little Sachi walk quietly up to her baby brother, put her face close to his and say quietly, "Baby, tell me what God feels like. I'm starting to forget."

Dan Millman

"You mean I do the Hokie Pokie and I turn myself around,
and that's what it's all about?"

Permissions

We would like to acknowledge the following publishers and individuals for permission to reprint the following material. (Note: The stories that are public domain or were written by Jack Canfield, Mark Victor Hansen or Patty Hansen are not included in this listing. Also, those stories that were penned anonymously, or by an unknown author, are not included. We have exercised due diligence but failed to locate the copyright holders of these stories. If you have any information concerning the copyrights of these stories, please contact us.)

At the end of each entry, we have listed the book and page(s) from which the story was taken: *Chicken Soup for the Soul* (CSSI); *A 2nd Helping of Chicken Soup for the Soul* (CSSII); or *A 3rd Serving of Chicken Soup for the Soul* (CSSIII).

Recognize Your Winners. Reprinted by permission of *Speaker's Idea File* by Don Martin, *Team Think: Using the Sports Connection to Develop, Motivate, and Manage a Winning Business Team.* ©1993 Dutton. *CSSIII, pp. 102-103.*

Be Yourself. Reprinted with permission of Pam Finger and Erik Oleson. ©1993 Pam Finger and Erik Oleson. *CSSII, p. 28.*

I Like Myself Now from *Man, The Manipulator* by Everett L. Shostrom. Used by permission. ©1967 Abingdon Press. *CSSI, p. 124.*

Ask for Appreciation. Excerpted from *The Best of Bits and Pieces.* Reprinted by permission of Economics Press. ©1994 Economics Press.

Nothing but the Truth! Reprinted by permission of David Casstevens. *CSSI, pp. 73-75.*

Our Deepest Fear. Reprinted by permission of Marianne Williamson. From the book *A Return to Love,* by Marianne Williamson ©1992. *CSSIII, p. 232.*

Tommy's Essay. Reprinted by permission of Jane Lindstrom. ©1975 Jane Lindstrom. *CSSIII, pp. 79-80.*

The Gift of the Gods. Reprinted by permission of Renee R. Vroman. ©1995 Renee R. Vroman. (Originally printed under the title of *The Gift.*) *CSSIII, pp. 110-111.*

But You Didn't. Reprinted by permission of Stan Gebhardt. ©1994 Stan Gebhardt. *CSSII, p. 94.*

HEALTH COMMUNICATIONS, INC. TITLES
BY JACK CANFIELD AND MARK VICTOR HANSEN

BOOKS

Chicken Soup for the Soul™
A 2nd Helping of Chicken Soup for the Soul™
Chicken Soup for the Soul Cookbook *(with Diana von Welanetz Wentworth)*
The Master Motivator *(Mark Victor Hansen and Joe Batten)*
A 3rd Serving of Chicken Soup for the Soul™
Chicken Soup for the Surviving Soul *(with Nancy Mitchell and Patty Aubery)*
Condensed Chicken Soup for the Soul™ *(with Patty Hansen)*
A Cup of Chicken Soup for the Soul™ *(with Barry Spilchuk)*
Chicken Soup for the Woman's Soul *(with Jennifer Read Hawthorne and Marci Shimoff)*
Chicken Soup for the Soul at Work *(with Maida Rogerson, Martin Rutte and Tim Clauss)*

AUDIOS

Chicken Soup for the Soul™ 3-Volume Audiotape Gift Set
The Best of the Original Chicken Soup for the Soul™ *(tape and CD)*
The Best of A 2nd Helping of Chicken Soup for the Soul™ *(tape and CD)*
The Best of A 3rd Serving of Chicken Soup for the Soul™ *(tape and CD)*
Chicken Soup for the Woman's Soul *(tape and CD)*
Chicken Soup for the Soul at Work *(tape and CD)*

Tiny Treasures to Warm Your Heart

Condensed Chicken Soup for the Soul™
Jack Canfield, Mark Victor Hansen and Patty Hansen

Savor the heartwarming goodness of the *Chicken Soup for the Soul* series in this delightful collection of 101 inspirational gems. The very best short stories are concentrated here in one delectable little volume. This quick pick-me-up makes a marvelous bedside companion or pocketbook reader.

Code 4215 . . . . $8.95

A Cup of Chicken Soup for the Soul™
Jack Canfield, Mark Victor Hansen and Barry Spilchuk

New York Times bestselling authors Jack Canfield and Mark Victor Hansen join forces with Barry Spilchuk to serve you a brand-new collection of single-serving-sized *Chicken Soup for the Soul* stories. Chock-full of timeless wisdom and insightful cartoons, you're sure to find delight in each and every page of this little treasure.

Code 4215 . . . . $8.95

Available at your favorite bookstore or call 1-800-441-5569 for Visa or MasterCard orders.
Prices do not include shipping and handling. Your response code is CDCS.